JESUS AND THE GANG

JESUS AND THE GANG

YOUTH VIOLENCE AND CHRISTIANITY
IN URBAN HONDURAS

JON WOLSETH

The University of Arizona Press   Tucson

The University of Arizona Press
© 2011 The Arizona Board of Regents

www.uapress.arizona.edu

Library of Congress Cataloging-in-Publication Data

Wolseth, Jon, 1975–
    Jesus and the gang : youth violence and Christianity in urban
Honduras / Jon Wolseth.
        p.   cm.
    Includes bibliographical references and index.
    ISBN 978-0-8165-2908-7 (cloth : alk. paper)
        1. Youth and violence—Honduras—Case studies.
2. Gangs—Honduras—Case studies.   3. Youth—Religious
life—Honduras—Case studies.   4. Church and social
problems—Honduras—Case studies.   I. Title.
    HQ799.2.V56W65   2011
    303.60835'097283–dc22   2010033682

Manufactured in the United States of America on acid-free,
archival-quality paper containing a minimum of
30% post-consumer waste and processed chlorine free.

16   15   14   13   12   11   6   5   4   3   2   1

For my parents, Gary and Sharon Wolseth

Contents

List of Illustrations   ix

Acknowledgments   xi

1 Youth and the Politics of Violence in Honduras: The Murder of El Títere   1

2 Contesting Neighborhood Space in Colonia Belén   27

3 Thick as Blood: Street Ties, Gang Tattoos, and Graffiti   50

4 The Making of Community and the Work of Faith   72

5 Finding Sanctuary: Youth Violence and Pentecostalism   102

Conclusion: Taking on Violence   129

Appendix of Names   139

Notes   143

References   145

Index   153

Illustrations

1. Young men hanging out in front of a *pulpería*   20
2. Bridge, ravine, and Catholic church in Colonia Belén   28
3. Gang graffiti with gang members' nicknames   41
4. Second station of the cross for Good Friday procession   44
5. A young man getting his tattoos removed   63
6. Tombstone graffiti of the 18th Street Gang   68
7. Calling members to a Pentecostal church service   103

Acknowledgments

In the process of researching and writing this book, I have incurred many debts. First and foremost, I extend my gratitude to my friends and neighbors in Colonia Belén. I hope that my presentation does justice to the lives of the young men and women who made me part of their social world and offered me all manner of emotional and physical support. Their willingness to open up to me is what has made this work possible. I regret that I cannot mention them by name.

This project was funded through a Wenner-Gren Dissertation Fieldwork Grant, a University of Iowa Stanley Research Grant, a UI Student Government Research Grant, and the University of Iowa Department of Anthropology. Writing was partially funded by a Seashore-Ballard Fellowship. Some parts of this book are revised from previous publications. Parts of chapter 1 appeared in my article "Everyday Violence and the Persistence of Grief: Wandering and Loss among Honduran Youths," *Journal of Latin American and Caribbean Anthropology* 13, no. 2 (2008): 311–335. A shorter version of chapter 5 was published as my article "Safety and Sanctuary: Pentecostalism and Youth Gang Violence in Honduras," *Latin American Perspectives* 35, no. 4 (2008): 96–111.

Fieldwork was not always an easy venture. I thank the Beasley family for introducing me to El Progreso and their family, and thank Olivia for setting my mom's mind at ease. While living in El Progreso, I received daily support from the Rivas-Baquedano family, without whose encouragement and orientation I would have been completely lost. Allan Palma served as my confessor and confidant in the times I faced ethical and emotional dilemmas. Without him and his kind words of encouragement, I would have lost sight about what it was that I *was* doing. Father Melo and the social research team E.R.I.C. (Equipo de Reflexión, Investigación, y Comunicación) provided me with office space and instant colleagues. I formulated many of my initial ideas in discussions with Marlon Carranza, Misael Castro, and Marco Tulio Gómez. Their interest in my work, critical questions, and feedback were invaluable as

I worked through my field experiences. The Marcia and Carlos Flores family played gracious hosts while I was in Tegucigalpa. Antonio Young and family provided perspective and opened many doors. Daisy Aracely Girón transcribed the interviews with care and precision. Regina Hausch spent many hours working with me on translations of my interviews. Without her assistance the translations would have sounded wooden and lifeless.

I profited from many hours of discussion, both in and out of the classroom, with colleagues at Iowa. Jacqueline Comito gave me direction, food for thought, and unswerving emotional support (and even a roof over my head at a critical moment!) throughout all phases of research and writing. This work would have taken twice as long to finish and been only half as good had it not been for her encouragement and tough love. Special thanks goes to Jerry Wever, Betty Rodriguez-Feo, Samantha Solimeo, Ernie Cox, Sarah Ono, Carrie Hough, Brandy Case Haub, Mike Dunne, Steve Tulley, Murli Natrajan, and Vidya Kalaramadam for allowing me to sound off from time to time, and for providing intellectual stimuli and numerous fruitful directions for thinking about my data. At Luther College, my ideas continued to develop with the thoughtful comments and assistance of Harv Klevar, Tom Blanton, Amanda Hamp, Lea Pickard, Anne-Marine Feat, Amy Weldon, Matt Simpson, and Eric Baack. They represent the best of the liberal arts tradition of critical inquiry across the disciplines. Finally, presentation of various versions of the chapters collected herein has benefited from readings and reactions by Luther students both in and out of the classroom, especially those who have participated in my Street Cultures class. In particular, I would like to thank Greg Shirbroun for his editing assistance, and Chelle Meyer for her administrative assistance.

Florence Babb is a model academic advisor and scholar. Engaged with and supportive of my project from the start, she maintained concern throughout, while allowing me the freedom to explore and express my ideas. She was even supportive when I announced a two-and-a-half-year moratorium on the academy to join the Peace Corps. I owe an intellectual debt to Mac Marshall, Laura Graham, Rudi Colloredo-Mansfeld, Daniel Balderston, and Thomas A. Lewis. Conversations with each of them at various stages of the project proved to bear fruit. I hope they find some of their concerns in the end product.

Longtime friends are indispensable support, especially when you find yourself feeling isolated from the familiar. During fieldwork, I relied on my friends to keep me anchored and provide me with perspective. Jordan Sher came for a visit at a crucial time. Alexandra Graham kept faithful correspondence and aided from afar in an emergency. Hillery Pastovich, Tim Cravens, Chris Farley, Phil Decker, and Ted and Stephanie Gould were all sounding boards and supportive friends that could see through my bravado. Thank you all for being there throughout the years; I wouldn't be who I am without you.

A special thank-you goes to my family. My father, Gary, has always offered me enthusiastic support to follow my desires, while also being the voice of practical reason. My mother Sharon's encouragement and energy set the ball rolling, but it is her goodhearted concern that helped sustain this project. My sister, Kari Hamilton, always knew just what kind of support I needed—be it material or emotional. David Bordewyk offered his interest in my work, listened to my stories, and harbored a poor graduate student for extended periods of time. I relied on them to remind me of my place in the world. Finally, this project grew as my niece, Isabel, also grew. When trying to deal with the conflicting emotions of fieldwork and the pains of writing, she offered extended periods of play and wonder at the world to set me back on track.

JESUS AND THE GANG

1

Youth and the Politics of Violence in Honduras
The Murder of El Títere

Fieldnotes, September 29, 2001. I felt defeated, tired and worn out from
the day and it was only two o'clock in the afternoon. All morning long,
I had waited in that cramped, airless room at the municipal building in
the hopes of talking to someone, anyone, about the city's youth policy.
Instead, I came to understand what most other Progreseños already
knew: city officials have little time to recognize your existence if it is not
immediately beneficial to them. Hungry and discouraged, I headed back
to the neighborhood with the overwhelming feeling that I had gotten
absolutely nowhere today.

The bus was jammed full, as usual. By the time I got off at my stop,
sweat soaked through the cotton button-down from the crush of human
bodies and the intolerable heat and humidity of the outside air. I only
wanted to shower, to wash my stink away.

I could hear the young children hollering as I rounded the corner of
the dirt street where I lived. "*El muerto, el muerto,*" they cried, running
past me, toward the ravine as their mothers chased after them. *El muerto,*
I thought, *a dead body.* I caught Carlitos,[1] a kid of about twelve who lives
up the street from me, and asked him about all the excitement.

"They shot him, they shot El Títere," Carlitos hissed out in a short
breath. "El Títere is dead."

Carlitos wouldn't waste time explaining to me who El Títere is—or
rather, who he was. Agitated and excited, his sandaled feet were going to
fly away without him if he didn't get moving.

"Where are you going?" I called out after him.

"To go see the body," he cried, over his shoulder. He sank into the
ravine, crossing to the other side of the neighborhood. Forgetting my
weariness, I joined the flow of neighbors heading in that direction, not
believing what Carlitos told me. He must have gotten it wrong, or maybe
I'd misunderstood. There wouldn't be a dead body.

The street intersected perpendicularly with the ravine. As I climbed up
the steep side, I could see a large crowd shaped like a horseshoe, gathered

in front of a small, turquoise-colored cinder-block house. Lying parallel to the front door, just outside the threshold, was el muerto.

El Títere was shirtless, very thin, and barely twenty. Scribbled on the bare arm exposed to the crowd were tattoos proclaiming his allegiance to the 18th Street Gang. A large Gothic number 18 adorned his chest. Shot as he had been through the left cheek, the bullet had caused significant disfigurement to his face. Someone had placed a pillow under his head. His eyes, open and facing the crowd, had a glazed-over look.

His traumatized body referenced the only other freshly dead body I had ever seen. Driving home on the highway late one night in suburban Denver, my friends and I encountered a body lying extended in the middle of the right lane. In our disbelief and curiosity, we pulled over and directed traffic around the dead young man. Someone remembered to phone the police, and within ten minutes the cops took over. It was only afterward, as we finished the drive in a silence punctuated with an occasional "My God" or a simple "How? Why?" that the shock set in and the anonymity of the encounter worried us. What was most troubling to us was not any evidence of trauma, which was minimal, but that he could have been any one of us: early twenties, middle-class, suburban, white.

Looking into El Títere's eyes, I became acutely aware that all of us stood watching and did nothing but witness the spectacle of his dead body. Why did no one act? Where were the police? Why did we all just look at the body?

El Títere's family positioned themselves against the front of the house. Some sat on a low bench, others stood. They were all on display as much as the dead body. In the doorway leaned an old woman in a pale blue printed skirt and a white T-shirt with the arms cut off to offer more room for her substantial size. She wore a kerchief on her head; threads of gray and black hair protruded from the sides. Her body slumped slightly, as if resigned to the scene before her. I learned later she was El Títere's grandmother.

The explanations of what happened all seem so matter-of-fact, so banal. It was not indifference, not really, but there was no indignation, either. Later, I asked an older woman, a neighbor of El Títere's grandmother, about the murder, and her reply was: "It is too bad that they shot him, but he was a gang member. I have sympathy only for the family."

From where I was standing in the crowd, I could see that some young men I had recently met had arrived. They stared intensely at El Títere's body for minutes at a time.

I was there for an hour, and the police still had not arrived. Frustrated by my inability to make sense of what happened, and ashamed that I did not move to help, I returned to my room. I took a bucket shower, to wash away not so much the sweat as the taint of inaction.

El Títere's murder occurred in the first month of my field research. At that time, I did not understand the apparent apathy and abject spectatorship of the crowd. Unfortunately, his murder was my introduction to the way youth violence operates in Honduras. I learned, for instance, that police presence is not a reassuring act of assistance to those in need; more often it reflects aggressive acts of patrolling and harassment. Comments like that of the neighbor are typical expressions of disgust and distrust of youth, made even by those with family members who may be involved in gang or violent activity. Because of El Títere's murder, I paid closer attention to what community members were saying about the status of youth in Honduras. At the national level, I tuned into a pervasive rhetoric about stopping urban crime that relied on arguments concerning the criminality of young men. The abstract category of "youth," I learned, is one laden with the burden of being perceived as one of the prime failures of the nation.

Nine months after El Títere's murder I interviewed Sergio, a young man of eighteen who lived and grew up in Colonia Belén.[2] Slowly, over the previous months, Sergio and I had gained each other's trust and confidence. I had watched him struggle as he attempted to leave gang life through conversion to Pentecostalism. Most of the time, as I listened to Sergio and other young men talk about their past and present, I felt as if I played dual roles of confessor and psychologist. I did not feel comfortable with these roles, and often their stories would move me to silence; I was unable to find the words with which to respond. This interview style, if it could be called that, had the effect of encouraging them to fill the silence with long stretches of narrative. They would speak and I would listen. I could never tell if they were relieved to have someone outside of their everyday lives with whom to talk about themselves or if they offered these stories as an explanation of how they wanted to portray themselves to me. It is most likely a combination of the two.

Sergio's Story

That evening, instead of going to church services together, Sergio and I had our first formal interview. We sat in the dark recesses of a friend's kitchen. The one low-hanging lightbulb cast an uneven glow onto the kitchen table. Sergio held the tiny lapel microphone tightly in his left hand as if it were the only thing that could pull him from his past. For the first time, Sergio recounted for me how his closest gang buddy had been gunned down by a rival gang in front of his buddy's house. Only then, despite my several months of interacting with Sergio, did I realize that the young man I had seen slain on the street had been Sergio's best friend.

"I remember when they killed El Títere," Sergio said through his teeth, "I remember we were going to the carnival with some young ladies to party it up, according to us. Well, at three, three-ten in the afternoon this Saturday, they are killing him, they are killing him, they killed him near his own house, they killed him in the gate to the house there. Why did they kill him? Because he said he was going to stay in the streets. And God proved him right. As [Títere] said, so God made it so, 'if he [Títere] was born for the streets, he's going to die in the streets.' Just like that." Sergio shifted in the kitchen chair, bowing his head to look at the tablecloth.

"They left him [Títere] lying there, by his own house, shirtless. They shot him seven times. I remember that the people there said that when they put the first [shot] in him he said, 'No, grandma. I left it [the gang],' he said, yelled that way, and he fell to the ground.

"He shot him once here," Sergio points to his stomach, "another here," he points to his cheek, "and he shot him more, so that Títere was shot seven times and he was crying, but even so he [Títere] stayed that way, see? That way with his hand," Sergio flashed the gang sign, writing the number eighteen with his fingers, "that way he [Títere] remained throwing the *Barrio* [giving the gang sign] then."

Sergio paused, drawing in his breath. The tape caught a heavy sigh. "He didn't want to pay attention, Títere." Sergio continued, "His mom is a *cristiana* (evangelical Christian), his mother's way of being is very beautiful. But what good did that do? Now that I walk in the path [of the Lord], she's really cool with me. The first day she saw me with the Bible, I started to cry with her; it was so emotional because when she saw me, 'Sergio,' she tells me, 'Come,' she tells me, and she hugged me and started to cry. And I started to think that if my mother was still alive she'd be happy, and I liked that thought.

"And she started to counsel me; she invited me to eat at her house. I went to eat and we were talking and she was crying, and I felt this thing here, an awful thing here in my throat, like I was going to cry. And she started to say to me, 'Don't go astray, don't go astray,' and crying she

[says] that she's going to support me in everything. And for this I asked God that he might help me, that he might give me more courage to continue, that I might not go astray."

For Sergio, El Títere's death was a clarion call. To me, it is also an entry point into social debates over youth violence in Honduras. In common with other youth, Sergio's struggle is one of defining the subjective and social self—how he understands himself and his place in the world. Despite his recent past involvement in violence as a perpetrator and victim, Sergio would like to redefine his life. The murder of his best friend was the catalyst of this desire. Yet Sergio realizes that the only way he can leave behind a social self as a gang member is through the acceptance of a new social self, that of being Pentecostal. Such a change is not easy and involves a knot of personal feelings as Sergio tries to integrate who he wants to be with who he was, as well as the social perceptions involved with his past and present behavior. It also involves a reworking of community and family relations. We see this as Sergio invokes the death of his mother and his ties to multiple sets of local communities, such as the church, his former gang, and the opinions of everyone else in the neighborhood. Violence has profoundly affected the social and psychological aspects of Sergio's life, conditioning his personal responses, as well as the way others in society behave toward him.

Sergio is an exemplar of the type of youth who cause the most anxiety for society—jobless, violent, and without the support of traditional institutions such as family and school. Such youths are signs for society; if they are out of control or in danger, so is the society that spawned them. Where youths are, whom they are with, and what they are doing are general concerns for most members of a society. Society raises these general concerns in debates over violence, high unemployment, exploitive work conditions, lack of opportunities for advancement, and an array of consumer goods tauntingly out of reach. In other words, when people talk about social problems, they invoke the status of youth as a diagnostic sign of where a society may be headed. When neighbors express that they have no sympathy for murdered youths, as the older woman did after El Títere's murder, they are playing into a wealth of sociopolitical debates. When the state sends armed police and military patrols to poorer neighborhoods to combat street crime, they too reinforce certain views about the condition of youth in the nation.

Violence, whether in the form of assault or of homicide, has become one of the defining features of growing up for the current generation of

Honduran youth. This book examines the ways that young men in the working-class and working-poor neighborhood of Colonia Belén in El Progreso, Honduras, respond to youth violence by drawing on the available social institutions present in their lives. Young men literally appropriate violent means to navigate social life, but they can also confront local violence by challenging the prevailing social logic that implicates all young men as perpetrators. In both senses, young men take on violence.

I discuss ways in which youths manage and contain violence in their community, through the mastery and manipulation of practices that neutralize potentially dangerous situations, people, and locales. Youths understand violence in particular ways that often cut across the grain of dominant, institutional understandings of why youth violence occurs. Concomitantly, members of society judge young people in relation to the degree that they conform to acceptable and expected mainstream cultural behavior. Youths, however, patch together ways of acting from preexisting expectations, creating new practices, which they view as having moral value. These practices draw upon the present social and institutional resources available, such as participation in local gangs and church organizations. Some young men consequently manipulate these resources by utilizing three kinds of cultural practices, which they implement to counter the effects of youth violence. First, youth occupy and appropriate geographical and metaphoric spaces in their community. Second, by occupying their time in a variety of pursuits—be it attending church services, working, continuing their education, or hanging out on street corners—youth confirm and critique what adult society expects of them. Finally, through the telling and retelling of stories, youths attempt to manage their interpersonal relationships with other youths and with the institutions of gangs and churches in their neighborhood. These spatial, temporal, and narrative practices work in conjunction to provide some maneuvering on the part of neighborhood youths. They have developed these survival strategies for living in an uncertain social environment.

In Honduras, gun violence disproportionately affects young men. In particular, working-class and working-poor young men have a violent public identity because of a highly publicized involvement in gangs. As both victims and perpetrators, young men are central to issues of gun violence in the country. To explore the effects of gun violence in the lives of youth, I conducted twelve months of ethnographic research and participant-observation in the working-class neighborhood that I call Colonia Belén. Although young men are central to concerns of gun violence, the opinions and experiences of young women help highlight practices specific to young men and offer commentary on the social consequences of youth violence in general. Therefore, I include research material from both young men and women. Gun violence may have an immediate impact on the bodies of young men, but young women are their sisters, girlfriends, wives, and friends. It is especially the young women involved in local church institutions who help to construct understandings of what types of support are available to young men. Together, young men and women define the range of what they deem as appropriate behaviors and attitudes for young men.

From the research material, I draw out the everyday options exercised by young men and the ways in which they negotiate a social reality that threatens young lives. Both media portrayals and social policy venues portray young men as the primary perpetrators of crime and gun violence and the cause of citizen insecurity. This dominant commonsense understanding of why youth violence occurs circulates in the country and makes logical social sense for the majority of Hondurans. It pervades most social institutions, even those few that offer themselves as resources for youth. In the working-poor barrios of urban areas, there is little presence of government or nongovernmental organizations. Local churches, both Catholic and evangelical Protestant, have stepped in as the primary guides for young men and women. Churches, however, still work within the general framework of looking at young men as a population that needs to be socially and religiously redeemed for the sake of the nation.

If the ideological and practical forces of social institutions reinforce the idea of a lost generation of young men, youths have developed a set of countervailing practices to make themselves heard and seen. Although they draw on the institutional formulations that rationalize youth violence, these practices twist dominant meanings and re-present young men's behavior as one of the few self-affirming options available to them. While the Honduran state offers little practical support to increase future possibilities for low-income youth, youth develop their own methods to memorialize their experiences, preserve their existence, and maneuver through social violence.

To understand these countervailing practices, I call on a diverse set of theoretical perspectives to illuminate the ways that young men assert their own existence in light of pervasive gun violence. In doing so, I emphasize that they act in calculating ways that allow them to draw on the moral power of institutions when they need to, even while they may at other times act in ways that challenge these very same institutions. It is in this realm of appropriation and deployment that de Certeau's focus on the tactics of everyday life (1984) allows us to recognize the malleability of social life and the resilience of social actors. However, before his death, de Certeau provided us with only a limited set of examples (reading, walking, and cooking) from which to understand how social actors exercise agency in the face of the homogenization of social institutions. To apply his perspective to novel situations, I draw on other social theorists whose work speaks more directly to the problems at hand.

The management of violence requires an intimate knowledge of social and spatial relations. One way in which youth navigate the immediate violence in their neighborhood is through developing a sense of place. Lefebvre's (1991) conceptualization of social space—that social relations intimately connect with spatial relations—is useful for understanding how young men and women move about within communities. I explore the tension between the efforts of the local branch of the 18th Street Gang and church institutions to memorialize violent places in Colonia Belén. In this instance, churches seek to homogenize an understanding of community violence and thus present a particular interpretation of youth violence. Gang youth, on the other hand, mark out the social space of the neighborhood as being congruent with the gang, through the use of graffiti and other signifying practices. Creatively manipulating social and spatial relations, youth, regardless of institutional affiliation, stress alternatives to their physical disappearance from public spaces.

Using graffiti, tattoos, and other signifying practices, the 18th Street Gang, La Mara Salvatrucha, and the Los Vatoslocos gang have a highly visible presence in working-poor neighborhoods in Honduras. Upon joining a gang, members align themselves with the identification of the corporate gang through developing intimate interpersonal relationships with another member. Known as *carnal* relationships, these not only act as a mentoring connection, but also as an effective way to control individual members within a less hierarchical gang structure. Borrowing from Vigil's (1988) concept of street socialization, I explore mechanisms such as tattooing, renaming, and the use of graffiti that facilitate the socialization process and lead to an individual identification with the gang. In particular, writing practices such as tattooing and graffiti are exemplary illustrations of de Certeau's (1984) concepts of how social institutions claim possession of the individual.

Youths also respond to violence by drawing on the authority of social institutions such as churches. Through participation in Catholic or evangelical Christian churches, youth draw on the moral authority of these institutions and redeploy their messages and ideologies to develop unique responses to violence. I use two theoretical perspectives to examine more fully the competing ideologies of the Catholic and Pentecostal traditions. To understand the progressive Catholic Church's position of a theology of "accompaniment," I expand on Durkheim's concept of "moral communities" (1995). The Catholic Church's full embrace of the poor and disenfranchised creates a situation in which a Catholic's identification as a member of the dispossessed binds together the community. However, young men and women in the parish are aware that such identification puts them at risk of being mistaken for violent and drug-addicted youth.

Second, returning to Lefebvre (1991), I explore how Pentecostalism offers young men a sense of safety by providing actual and metaphorical sanctuary from youth-on-youth violence. One of Pentecostalism's main tenets is the assertion that Pentecostals are separate from the mundane world. Young men take this idea and expand upon it, making Pentecostals' claims to separation apply to young men who wish to remove themselves from the gang.

Sergio's internal dilemmas and Títere's murder occur within a political and social context in which juvenile crime and delinquency hold grave concern for the future of the nation. Children and youth are catalysts in government's reactions toward increased crime, insecurity, and failing economies. To best understand the sociopolitical context in which young men and women find themselves embroiled and constrained, we must examine the cultural politics of youth violence in the hemisphere.

The Cultural Politics of Youth Violence in the Americas

Youth and adolescence are as much social constructions as are gender, sexuality, and race. As Acland points out, "youth is not just a social category with particular forms of cultural expression and investment; it is also a conjunction point for various discourses with powerful implications for the forms and specificities of the popular at a given moment" (1995:10). In developing a cultural politics of youth, it is crucial to understand that the term has a shifting history with multiple meanings, depending upon the sociopolitical context in which it is found (Wolseth and Babb 2008). An emphasis on the social construction and specificity of the category "youth" parallels recent anthropological writings on the cultural politics of childhood (Malkii and Martin 2003; Scheper-Hughes and Sargent 1998; Stephens 1995a) that recognize social anxieties about the condition of children as productive realms of inquiry. Stephens's pioneering work (1995b), for instance, demonstrated that social policies concerning children are often enacted in response to debates about ethnic conflict, nationalism, and cultural autonomy. Stephens called for researchers to direct attention to the socially contingent category of "child" and to recognize that state-level policies directed at children reflect the moral concerns of society.

In Central America, concerns about male youth in the public arena link primarily with the moral panic (Cohen 1972) of gang violence. Youths are made to shoulder the blame for the rising sentiment of citizen insecurity and the failure of democratic governance in the region (Rodgers, Muggah, and Stevenson 2008). For example, during the 2001 presidential campaign in Honduras, juvenile delinquency and the status of youth played a central role in all party platforms. Tellingly, the candidate who went on to win the election, Ricardo Maduro, employed a rhetoric of security and safety detailing "zero tolerance" for crime, especially gang violence. The emphasis on youth gangs in the country camouflages the high level of non-gang-related organized crime. At the same time, this emphasis ignores the needs of all youths in the country. In the process, strong-arm military tactics and punitive policies sweep aside broader economic and political development issues, including a consolidation of democracy (Rodgers 2007).

Structural adjustment policies and the servicing of Honduras's ballooning national debt eliminate the availability of funds to spend on social development issues for young people. During the decade of the 1990s, management of the foreign debt took precedence in federal budgets, even as the total debt increased by more than a third of what it had been in 1989. By the end of the decade, the country spent more servicing its $3.8 trillion external debt than on social services (Programa de las Naciones Unidas para el Desarrollo 1999:95). In other words, health and education programs are on the losing side, continually seeing their budgets whittled down to a skeletal existence, while military and police programs win the lion's share in the face of increased crime, delinquency, and citizen insecurity (Hernández, Posas, and Castellanos 2000). As a consequence, youth become part of an "unknown" sector of the general population in terms of public policy (Lanza 2002:6–7). Youths are effectively erased from political plans for human and economic development, experiencing social exclusion to the point of disappearance (Krauskopf 1998). This disappearance of youth from social programming combines with the more familiar form of disappearance in Latin America and Honduras—the disappearance of the physical body through kidnapping and murder. The coincidence is striking.

In Honduras, the implementation of structural adjustment policies relies on military and police intervention into civil society (Ruhl 2000). This is the latest in a long history in the country of the use of authoritarianism to direct economic and labor policies (Euraque 1996; Morris 1984; Pine 2008). The structural effects of capitalism reverberate throughout the social and political bodies to the most micro level, that of individuals who live their lives within the constraints of political economy. It would not go too far to suggest that neoliberal economic policies mark the physical body, inscribing suffering on bodies by altering physical appearance through hunger, disease, and, most dramatically, scars, permanent injury, and death that are the results of violence. In particular, high rates of youth violent death have detrimental effects on the vitality of the social body. The bodily evidence of youth violence, however, "offer[s] practical signs that demand being read as a commentary on the regulation of citizens' rights" (Rotker 2002:18). Indeed, the bodies of young men act as a palimpsest of the state's failure to provide for its young. At a time when public funding for youth—specifically educational funding and job training—is disappearing from budgets, youth are disappearing from social life through their murders.

The decade of the 1990s and the first years of the twenty-first century have been marked by rising violent death and murder rates throughout the Western Hemisphere (World Health Organization 2002). The trend is pronounced in the Americas, where, with the exception of Canada, violent death and murder rates have eclipsed the previous high-water marks of the late 1970s and 1980s. Even countries that were in the throes of civil war in the 1980s—such as Nicaragua, El Salvador, Guatemala, and Peru—have seen violent death rates increase exponentially. Since that time, in the Americas as a whole, men between fifteen and twenty-nine years old have been more likely to die by violent means than has any other age or gender combination, with a rate of eighty-three deaths per 100,000 (ibid.).

These statistics are telling, because they demonstrate that there is a pattern to the targets for most murders in the Americas, targets that are based on definable social characteristics such as age, gender, and class. When we compare the statistics for violent death rates with population percentages, we find that violent death is widespread among one of the smallest population subgroups in the Americas, the young men who make up 10 percent of the population in the Americas and 45 percent of all violent death cases (World Health Organization 2002). This number is dramatically disproportionate to the population of young men within the hemisphere. The trend for the region is consistent for individual nations. According to human rights activists in Honduras, young men ages twelve to twenty-four, who account for 14 percent of the population, were victims in 1,700 murder cases in 2001 (Umanzor 2002:31). This number represents nearly 73 percent of the 2,342 violent deaths recorded by the national police that same year (Girón 2002:4).

Unfortunately, the rise in violent death among youth points to an increased weakness in governance in the region. Despite Central America's post–civil war democratic transition in the 1990s, investment in the well-being and inclusion of young people has not been a priority in the region. Crime and policing efforts have been the primary social policies funded, instead of a focus on programs that could potentially increase the life opportunities of youth, such as education reform or job training. Indeed, the cultural politics of youth in Central America centers on controlling and demobilizing the violent young male offender.

The financial squeeze and individualism of recent economic policies are accentuated by several consequences of the Central American conflicts and the use of Honduras as a de facto U.S. military base in the 1980s (LaFeber 1993; LeoGrande 1998). First, the presence of U.S. military advisors in Honduras created an environment in which authoritarian and strong-arm tactics became the norm for the Honduran military and national police (not separate entities until the 1990s). Recently declassified CIA papers reveal that the U.S. ambassador—and later U.N. ambassador—John Negroponte had urged the use of so-called dirty-war tactics by military authorities against the Honduran populace. He had contracted with Argentine military officials to train and support the Honduran military (Lanza and Peacock 2000). Such training and recourse to dirty-war tactics by military and police personnel are still in use in contemporary Honduras in the form of extrajudicial execution-style murders of poor and homeless young men and children (Campbell

2003; Harris 1997; Lanza 2002). Adorno, discussing the rise of crime and crime prevention in São Paulo, identifies major consequences of the "militarization of public security" (2002:150). In such situations, common crime morphs into "an internal security problem," which confuses "control of the general public and the control of national security" (ibid.). In a related fashion, the methods employed by Honduran security forces to alleviate crime have become increasingly patterned after military rules of engagement. As such, gangs are the new "enemy," since they pose a threat to the state's control of power (see Moser and Rodgers 2005).

As a major component of President Maduro's "zero tolerance" crime policy, the joint police and armed forces units patrol poorer, "gang-infested" neighborhoods in urban Honduras. These patrols are a visible manifestation of this conflation of public and national security. Units of five to ten special forces members, called Cobras, scour neighborhoods looking for "the enemy," now the *marero*, or gang member. Mareros, who are private citizens, have become enemies of the state and are construed as a threat to national security. Being treated as a threat to the nation by security forces opens the door for aggressive, dehumanizing methods of surveillance and control, which, in effect, strip mareros and other young men of their citizen status. Consequently, they are treated as less than human and disenfranchised from state-approved channels of mediation such as the justice system and social services.

Second, the Central American peace accords and subsequent disarmament did not anticipate the degree to which weaponry would flow from rebel groups, paramilitaries, and military institutions into the hands of private citizenry (Castellanos 2000; Godnick, Muggah, and Wasznick 2002). As a result, the prevalence of unregistered private arms is commonplace and perpetuates vigilante justice. In other words, where an abusive and ineffective police force exists, it should be no surprise that private citizens take justice into their own hands. Many of the arms that are used by "juvenile" gangs and "adult" bandits are holdovers from this period. This also explains why access to, and use of, heavy weaponry—semiautomatic and automatic machine guns such as AK-47s and Uzis, grenades, and the occasional bazooka—by criminal groups supplements the much more common use of a variety of pistols, shotguns, and homemade handguns, or *chimbas*.

One result of the system of economic market competition is that it has opened up new avenues for redistributing the wealth of the nation through the use of armed banditry. Criminal competition, with other criminals and with security forces, requires ever-larger resources of guns and ammunition to continue and guarantee successful operation. The illegal arms market is a flourishing business that defies regulation and further draws resources away from the state (even while agents of the state may participate in the market for their own personal gain).

As should be clear by now, governmental policy choices force federally funded programs for youth to run on bare-bones budgets. Indeed, one observer of Honduran electoral politics since the transfer from military to civilian rule remarks:

> Honduras is hardly a model democracy. The performance of elected democratic governments has fallen far short of public expectations. Most public officials have concentrated on capturing the legal and illegal spoils of office for themselves and their political networks rather than on addressing the needs of one of the poorest populations in the Americas. Neoliberal economic reforms have yet to improve the lives of the underprivileged majority. (Ruhl 2000:525; see also Schulz and Schulz 1994)

Corruption, mismanagement of public funds, and reliance on the military as the prime political actor combine to disenfranchise the majority of Hondurans from political and economic life and erode the foundations of civil society. Even historically favored public organizations such as the military and police have experienced crucial budget cuts that make them ineffective as managers of public safety and enforcers of public laws. An admixture to this is a justice system that is corrupt, overworked, and impossibly flawed. When added together, an ineffectual judiciary and a visible yet tenuous public safety program is a recipe for public distrust of justice and law enforcement, just two more sources fostering the growth of youth violence. All of this creates a social environment that fosters the acceptance of vigilante justice at the local level.

Shrinking states, the disappearance of social welfare systems, and violence and conflict are political economic realities for many young people the world over. They are critical integers in an equation adversely affecting their health and safety. Children and youth experience and comprehend the political and economic contexts in which they live from their own points of view. Yet we must take the additional step of examining the *actions* of young people, as well as their thoughts and perceptions, to comprehend children and youth as creative agents. While in the field, I could not help but see young people as active decision makers who affected their immediate social worlds—the family, household, and city where they live. Again, using Sergio as an example of such decision making, we can see that youth are aware of the institutional resources available to them, and the options they have in developing responses to violence in their communities. Sergio understood that his primary resources were either with an evangelical church or with the gang. His was a decision of choosing between opposing social groups, the more normative church group or the antisocial position he already occupied.

Youth make choices about whether to follow social norms or challenge them and be labeled as deviant. Social deviance is not solely a psychological phenomenon based on the socialization of "problem youth" but also highlights political-economic factors that might influence the types of choices youth have. So-called social deviance can "be understood not simply as culture-specific manifestations of psychological distress, but more importantly as critical cultural practices through which young people display agency" (Bucholtz 2002:531). We can understand so-called deviant behavior as resistance to hegemonic cultural norms and an assertion of youth agency in the manufacturing of meaning in their lives. The emphasis on youth's cultural production and cultural practices "foregrounds age not as trajectory" but age as an identity, which "is agentive, flexible, and ever-changing" (ibid.:532). Focusing on youth as identity asserts that young people shape their present world, are social actors in their own right, even—or especially—in the face of violence and social exclusion. Any understanding of youth must start from their own perspective. Even if young men and women behave in ways that place themselves at greater risk of disease, bodily harm, or altercations with the law, we must engage with how youth view their own behavioral choices in the face of a political-economic context that may heavily delimit the choices they are able to make. The young men and women with whom I worked and lived in El Progreso, Honduras, are exemplars of young people who actively create meaning and community in violent times. To better understand their lives, I now turn to a brief description of El Progreso and the primary community where I worked, Colonia Belén.

El Progreso, Honduras, as Field Site

Honduras and the city of El Progreso are, in many ways, an ideal setting for examining the way youth creatively utilize institutional resources to offset the effects of social violence. A nation rooted in the mono-crop agricultural exploitation of the late 1800s and early 1900s—Honduras has the dubious distinction of being the "original banana republic"—many of the post-1950s social and economic structural transitions exemplify regional trends in demographics and economic policies. Rapid urbanization in the country clearly demonstrates how a decrease in mono-crop prices (primarily bananas and coffee in Honduras) energizes rural–urban migration. This process was hastened by additional extranational forces.

By the 1980s, part of the "benefits" of being a U.S. military base and staging ground for the clandestine Contra War in Nicaragua included the courting of U.S. manufacturing companies to the country. Thus began a nascent *maquila* industry to supplement agro-exports. In exchange for industrial "investment" in the form of light manufacturing, Honduras offers multinational corporations exemption from corporate taxation, a ready labor pool, and a history of strong-arm military repression of labor movements. High unemployment and underemployment rates reinforce the ready labor pool for the manufacturing sectors. Hurricane Mitch in 1998 retarded agricultural production, especially in bananas and palm oil, hastening rural out-migration and an ever-steady rise in unemployment.

Although not a large country in terms of population (just slightly over six million people), statistically Honduras demonstrates many prevailing trends for the whole of Latin America: an urban population that makes up nearly half of the national total, with almost 62 percent of the population under the age of twenty-five. The industrial and manufacturing corridor on the north coast Valle de Sula region contains a chain of medium-sized cities connected by shared infrastructure and a historical relationship with the banana industry (Euraque 1996). This cluster includes San Pedro Sula, the largest urban area other than the capital, along with smaller urban areas such as Villanueva, La Lima, Choloma, and El Progreso, all within an hour's bus ride of one another. This corridor consists of an archipelago of free trade zones, and the banana, African palm, and sugar cane fields are dotted with maquila manufacturing compounds.

El Progreso, compared to the cities on the north coast with colonial histories, is a recent construction, formally incorporated in 1892. The city is very much an outgrowth of agricultural production on the north coast, even having at one time been the home of United Fruit Company's Honduran Headquarters (Municipalidad de El Progreso 1998).

Throughout much of the twentieth century, El Progreso was nothing more than a service center for the surrounding agricultural villages. The population grew little, hovering under 25,000 people until the early 1970s. A restructuring of the banana industry, along with the shrinking importance of sugar cane production on the world market, led to an influx of rural migrants looking for work. The city was unable to accommodate the population explosion. El Progreso grew too fast. None of the needed infrastructure accompanied the demographic shift in the city. The municipality did not lay water and sewer pipes as new neighborhoods sprang up. Thirty years later, outside of the paved downtown area of the city, the dirt streets are washboarded and punctuated with potholes. Urban expansion has continued without consistent municipal planning and leadership. The city grows despite the absence of constant water supply, sewer treatment, and trash removal.

Although banana, palm oil, and sugar cane production are still important agricultural economic activities, El Progreso has transformed itself over the last twenty years into a peri-urban industrial site. Light manufacturing has had a great impact on the local economy. Although El Progreso has only one industrial park within city limits, many industrial parks exist between El Progreso and nearby San Pedro Sula. Both draw from El Progreso's workforce. El Progreso has the feel of a bedroom community, because many people commute daily to San Pedro Sula, a city of a half million people, where they work, attend university, and shop. For a city of 85,000, El Progreso faces many of the same challenges as larger urban areas, partly because of its close proximity to San Pedro Sula. Rapid urban growth, unemployment, petty crime, and gun violence are prevalent in a city where the local government lacks the economic resources with which to supply even the most basic infrastructure, much less address these more complex social problems. Hurricane Mitch only exacerbated and amplified these problems for El Progreso. Consequently, urban crime, including homicide, is a grave concern for the city and the rest of the Valle de Sula corridor. Newspaper accounts, politicians, and locals alike commonly characterize this area as "crime infested," "filled with gangs," or "most dangerous." Young men are consistently implicated as the source of violent crime.

Colonia Belén is a neighborhood of six hundred houses located approximately five miles to the south and east of the downtown area. A product of the initial phase of urban expansion, Belén is one of El Progreso's more established neighborhoods. The neighborhood began as a

Jesuit-funded disaster-relief project in 1974, a result of Hurricane Fifi. The plan was to offer low-payment mortgages to working-poor inhabitants over a twenty-year period. With the help of Canadian and Dutch nongovernmental organizations (NGOs), the Jesuits built four hundred single-room, prefabricated wood-frame houses. The priest who had initiated the project came to feel that community members who refused to pay the agreed-upon low monthly mortgage had violated his goodwill. Some neighborhood members jokingly claim that this was the beginning of Colonia Belén's bad reputation.

Over time, the neighborhood has slowly changed in significant ways. Of course, some original residents have moved out and new ones have moved in over the course of twenty-five years. Many in the neighborhood attributed a decrease of involvement in civic action and community service—cleaning up the ravine that bifurcates the neighborhood, filling ruts in the dirt streets, or setting up a community vigilance committee—to an increase of new residents who feel less invested in the community. Longtime residents recount proudly how they had managed to construct their neighborhood over time, bringing electricity and water service to each individual home, and petitioning for a municipal bus route. Perhaps, they often conclude, now that so many struggles have been fought, people are more interested in themselves and not so much in their neighbors' well-being.

In addition to a demographic transition, the neighborhood has experienced cosmetic changes. It is rare today to see an original development project house standing. The development plan had included enough lot space so that many owners have added onto their homes over time, either placing concrete block additions onto the original wood structure or building over the original foundation altogether. Many homes give the impression of being constantly under construction, since improvement projects depend upon available funds: stacked concrete blocks wait to become walls, wrought iron takes the place of wooden doors and window shutters. Work migration to the United States and family remittances have also made possible a new class of residence in the neighborhood, albeit still rare enough to give the passer-by pause. Large, newly constructed houses, sometimes taking up two lots, are constructed as a model home would be. They incorporate an indoor bathroom and kitchen, tiled floors and ceiling fans, and an imposing concrete and wrought-iron fence that surrounds the entire lot. Colonia Belén is experiencing a steady polarization of housing styles in which larger, more modern, more secure homes indicate the presence of family members living in the United States.

Despite its many years of existence, Colonia Belén has very few businesses operating within close distances. Instead, every street has multiple *pulperías*, small shops run from homes that sell everything from basic food staples such as beans and rice, to the ubiquitous Coke or Pepsi products, to cleaning supplies. Occasionally, fruit and vegetable vendors will drive through the neighborhood selling their goods from the back of pickup trucks with attached loudspeakers barking out what they are selling and for how much. For most goods and services, residents travel to downtown El Progreso or into San Pedro Sula, either because what they seek is unavailable in the neighborhood or is perceived as being cheaper elsewhere. In addition to a paucity of commercial sites, the neighborhood also has very few nighttime entertainment options: no discos, clubs, or movie theaters. All of these are located downtown, and even if the buses ran late at night, they would still be economically out of reach for many neighborhood residents. Belén does have a number of churches, drinking establishments (cantinas), and pool halls competing for clientele. It was within Colonia Belén that I developed my greatest understanding of the lives of young people. By watching and listening, asking questions and living among them, I learned what it means to be a young Honduran living in such circumstances.

Everyday Ethnography

The neighborhood of Colonia Belén provides the setting for those youth whose responses to gun violence shape the story I tell. It was in multiple neighborhood venues, such as homes, front stoops, churches, and street corners, that I shared in the rhythm of daily life. As a participant-observer, I engaged in an ongoing conversation about what it means to be young, urban, and poor in Honduras. During my year of fieldwork, I turned twenty-six years old, placing me toward the older end of the *joven*, or youth, age spectrum. This helped me significantly to gain rapport with young men and women, because, although I was definitely an "outsider" in terms of being from the United States, they viewed me as an "insider" as well, because of my age. Young men and women assumed that I shared certain elements of a common experience with them. Being an unmarried male who lived with a resident family in the neighborhood—and also therefore under the matriarch's household authority and responsible to

Figure 1. Young men hanging out in front of the *pulpería* at night. The gun is fake. Photograph by author.

her—I shared commonalities with many of the local young men. Concomitantly, my position as an American youth was the focus for comparisons between the "American" way and the "Honduran" way of being young.

In addition to weekly rounds of visiting youths in their homes, and meeting their parents or guardians, I also spent time on a daily basis with different groups of young men and women as they congregated on street corners, in front of pulperías, and on the sidewalks in front of people's houses (fig. 1). In these venues, young men and women talk among themselves about daily occurrences and past events, gossip about their friends and acquaintances, and express concern about local and national politics. Such discussions guided my thinking about the themes that I present in this book. Although I did not feel comfortable tape-recording these moments, I would later record them in my fieldnotes. All youth with whom I spent a good deal of time knew from the outset that I took notes about our conversations. Some requested to see my notebooks and would eagerly search out their names, ask me to explain what I had written, and then correct or affirm my memory of the event in question. And of course, people told me some things in confidence; these I did not record in my fieldnotes.

I also attended local church services and youth groups on a regular basis. Church participation is an integral part of many young people's lives and, as we shall see in the course of this book, it is an important resource for youth as they develop responses to violence. As in other urban neighborhoods throughout the country, church institutions have an active and visible presence within Colonia Belén.

Within the neighborhood, there is a Catholic church with a supportive congregation. A loyal, albeit small, core reflecting a cross section of the neighborhood regularly attended weekly services. This number was augmented considerably by the many people within the neighborhood who expressed to me that they are Catholic, but whom I saw attending services only sporadically. Associated with the Catholic church is a youth pastoral outreach that held biweekly meetings in a building owned by the parish. The youth group was organized in 1999 in conjunction with a novice in the Society for Jesus (the Jesuits). Over the three years that the group had existed, they expanded from a core membership of four to six to a regular membership of approximately thirty youth. Membership was fluid and many longstanding members who had not attended recently would make occasional appearances and were always readily welcomed. The meetings attracted a wide variety of youth, and the group was not limited to those Catholic youth who attended Mass regularly (see chapter 4).

The neighborhood, like the nation as a whole, also has the very vocal presence of evangelical churches of a variety of denominations: Pentecostal, Baptist, Evangelical Free, Seventh Day Adventist, Mormon, and Jehovah's Witness. Colonia Belén had six non-Catholic churches within the neighborhood. This number would jump to eleven if we included the churches on the immediate edges of the neighborhood. All members of these churches are popularly and collectively called *evangélicos*. Although I met youth from many of these churches and attended different services, I chose to study one Pentecostal church in particular, because of the rapid growth of its youth membership and the relatively high percentage of youth who held leadership positions within the church structure. All Honduran evangelical churches that I came to know shared a common insistence on the importance of youth conversion in the face of social problems. Pentecostal churches include *grupos de crecimiento,* or growth groups, that meet biweekly and whose purpose is to evangelize. Because of the evangelizing character of Pentecostalism, the church in Colonia Belén had more than twenty growth groups located throughout neighborhoods in El Progreso. I attended various growth groups that either had youth leadership or had a large youth membership. In addition to these biweekly meetings, I attended Sunday services and special weekly services organized and run by the youth or women's ministries, weekly prayer meetings, and monthly youth ministry meetings (see chapter 5).

At times, it seemed that religious meetings dominated my research life. During a typical week I found myself attending some sort of church-related activity, Pentecostal or Catholic, five or six nights a week. And then there were the "special" events that happened on a monthly basis: baptisms, church festivals, church-organized swim trips to the beach and, occasionally, to a large evangelizing campaign held in conjunction with international ministries. The youth who were active in religious events became my closest friends in the field. Although they spoke from a special position of deep involvement in their respective churches, these youth also shared many commonalities with other working-class and working-poor youth in Honduras. Their religious faith was but one lens (and not always the overriding one) through which they viewed political, economic, and cultural matters.

Through personal networks of young men and women, I also met a variety of youth who were not involved in Catholic or Pentecostal religious activities. Many times these were siblings, relatives, neighbors, and close friends of youths I already knew well. Over time, involvement with these additional youths provided a good counter to the young men and women I knew through religious activities. As my research wore on, I reserved nights during the week to spend with these other groups of youths who were often mixed along gender and religious lines.

Finally, as the impact of interpersonal violence in the lives of these youths became clear to me, I made a conscious effort to seek out those who were most often accused of being perpetrators of violent crime, mareros, or gang members. Many of the Pentecostal young men whom I befriended had been involved in a *mara*, or gang, earlier in their lives and had converted to Pentecostalism or another evangelical faith in order to leave the gang (see chapter 5). I owe much of my information about gangs and gang life to these young men, especially Sergio, whom I befriended as he struggled with that part of his life. I attempted to meet current gang members as well and was able to befriend a small number of them. However, soon after I began spending time with these young men, others in the community made clear to me that being seen publicly with them was not a good idea—as much for my own safety as for the harm done to my reputation. Out of fear that increased contact with mareros would close off many of the associations I had made in the community (especially with churches), I limited my contact with them, and, consequently, my ethnographic and interview data are not as rich in this area as they might otherwise have been. The community does not shun mareros per se; indeed, I found such individuals to be surprisingly well integrated into many aspects of neighborhood life as acknowledged "children of the neighborhood." Yet, as we shall see in the chapters that follow, youths must carefully negotiate their identities to avoid being classified as mareros.

In all, I recorded fifty-one in-depth, semistructured interviews with youth that cut across gender categories and the four groups outlined above—Catholic, Pentecostal, gang, and "nonaffiliated." These fifty-one youth represent only a fraction of the young men and women I met and with whom I became acquainted. Interviewed youth were chosen non-randomly by their willingness to be interviewed, their centrality to many of the narratives I heard circulating among youths, and their relationship with me. Without having had their confidence and trust, gained over many months of close contact, I would not have received the rich data presented here.

The youths I interviewed had their own reasons for wanting to be recorded. Some liked the idea of having their story placed in a book that would be read by others. For many of the Pentecostal youths, my project was seen as another form of evangelization, a reaching out to others in need of spiritual salvation. Some Catholic youths also saw interviews as an opportunity to provide a commentary on their faith. During some interviews, I sensed that the interest I took in their personal histories was in some way therapeutic for the young men and women. There is no doubt that the stories they recounted were told from their perspectives with their own interpretations of events. This is evident in how they told them to me—what parts were left in or out of the story. For this reason, I aimed to collect multiple perspectives on the same controversial events—whether they were local acts of violence, community action, church conversions, or a topic of general community gossip. It was because of my close involvement with youths that I was able to identify the types of stories circulating in the community and had youths retell the stories, with comments, specifically to me.

The stories that circulated among youth became my most valuable source of ethnographic material, because of the ways in which they

illuminated the interviews and placed young people's daily lives into
relief. For this reason, I frame each chapter with a narrative based on
my fieldnotes. These narratives set the tone for the material discussed
in the chapter by demonstrating how the theoretical concerns of the
anthropologist cannot be devoid of the practical concerns of the subjects
of ethnography. The framing narratives also provide insight into and
description of living conditions and the people that I could not include
elsewhere, thus enriching the ethnographic setting for readers.

I attempt to present a series of juxtaposed themes in what follows,
so that a multiplicity of perspectives emerge on the causes and effects
of youth violence. I wind together portions of interviews, fieldnote
excerpts, pieces of sermons and church meetings, public documents
such as governmental reports and newspaper articles, and my own analysis. I privilege the voices of young men and women throughout and rely
on their narrations to provide commentary on my analysis. To guide
the reader through the discussion of the many individuals introduced in
the narratives and interviews, I have included a list of names with brief
descriptions of age and background (see Appendix). Just as the youths
in Colonia Belén fashion a coherency (however provisional) out of violence by piecing together experience, events, and analysis, I have constructed my own coherency (just as provisional) of experience, events,
and analysis. As anthropologists, we are all "provisional tinkerers" in
this regard (Geertz 1995:20).

Organization of the Book

Chapter 2, "Contesting Neighborhood Space in Colonia Belén," more
fully introduces readers to the ethnographic setting of Colonia Belén
through the exploration of the efforts of neighborhood institutions to
contest the meaning of community places. Because the small bridge
that unites the two halves of the neighborhood was the site of multiple
gang shootings and police and vigilante patrols, it became the locus of
concern for many residents. The three main social institutions in the
neighborhood—members of the 18th Street Gang, the Catholic Church,
and various Pentecostal and evangelical churches—drew attention to the
bridge as a representation of the condition of youth in the neighborhood
and the nation. By participating in various commemorative practices
and ceremonies, young men and women in Colonia Belén affirm and
contest the position of being urban, poor, and young in Honduras.

In chapter 3, "Thick as Blood: Street Ties, Gang Tattoos, and Graffiti," I shift focus to explore the relationships among young male gang members in the 18th Street Gang. Moving beyond simple explanatory narratives of gang membership, this chapter delves into the experiential and embodied nature of street relationships, especially between *carnales*, or gang blood brothers. The chapter recounts the day in which Sergio, El Títere's *carnal*, is at the tattoo removal clinic, having agreed to have his tattoos removed. Sergio's tattoo of a clown face on his chest, done by El Títere, is similar to that which El Títere drew as graffiti on various neighborhood walls. Building on Vigil's (1988) insights that street socialization is a process by which family and institutional ties are replaced with gang ties, I demonstrate that tattoos done by peers and tombstone graffiti commemorating the death of members' gang buddies position the gang as the totality of the social world for young men who are gang members. The tattooed body and the graffitied wall become the same surface membrane, inscribing the gang's claim to possession of both. A seamless identity is drawn between the gang (El Barrio) and the neighborhood (el barrio) through the young men who make up both.

Youth are able to appeal to community protection through understandings of church doctrine. In particular, church metaphors of community and of sanctuary assist youths in responding to violence. In the next two chapters, I explore the spatial and spiritual claims of the Catholic and Pentecostal churches. In chapter 4, "The Making of Community and the Work of Faith," I detail how Catholic youth call for inclusion and reconciliation based on the common spatial identity of community in the hope of gaining forgiveness from community members. The opening narrative for the chapter recounts a Catholic Bible study meeting in which various gang members from the neighborhood participated. The ensuing discussion by members of the Catholic church tried, unsuccessfully, to draw the gang members under the sphere of influence of the greater community, thus making them part of, and not separate from, the lives of their neighbors. The Catholic Church, base ecclesiastical communities (CEBs), and Catholic youth groups provide an institutional framework that emphasizes the conjunction of faith, love, and work. I illustrate how youth employ an understanding of themselves as a moral community through the practice of their faith. Modeling their relationships with others on their relationship with God, Catholic youth approach violence by closing the distances between themselves and other youth.

By contrast, Pentecostal youth invoke exemption from violence through removing themselves from the community and carrying with them the rights to sanctuary. I begin chapter 5, "Finding Sanctuary: Youth Violence and Pentecostalism," with a description of a typical sermon by a Pentecostal pastor addressing youth violence through the need of youth to convert and hence be within the protection of both God and the church. In this chapter I analyze how the rhetoric and practice of Pentecostalism offers a break from community life. A doctrine of separation from community life also excludes Pentecostal youth from violent retribution, because they can appeal their rights to church sanctuary as long as they can effectively demonstrate their religious identity to others. A call to sanctuary is a move that allows many gang members temporarily to escape the violence of gang life by claiming privilege of protective space. Pentecostal conversion thus offers an option to reform one's own behavior that the greater community affirms.

Finally, in the concluding chapter, "Taking on Violence," I turn to the question of risk management and youth cultural practice by centering on the creative ways in which young men navigate social violence in their community. The chapter opens with a scene between two recently converted ex-gang members whose situations illustrate the difficulty of leaving behind those behaviors reflecting habits of violence. Even though youth demonstrate an ability to manage an unsafe environment, coping is no great measure of adjustment. Youth may be resilient, but that resiliency comes at the cost of dealing with the pain they experience at being subjected to physical and structural violence.

To better understand the impact of gun violence in the lives of youth, I now turn to an exploration of the local geography of that violence in Colonia Belén.

2
Contesting Neighborhood Space in Colonia Belén

The Drive-by Shooting at the Bridge

Just like people, places have reputations. The bridge over the ravine that bisects Colonia Belén is infamous in the city (fig. 2). Like so many other features of Belén, the bridge is diminutive in stature and structure, yet it has a much larger significance than its size warrants. As bridges go, this one is nothing special. Less than a hundred feet long, the low-lying floor supports a three-foot-high concrete railing. It is only wide enough for one vehicle at a time, and taxis have sparring matches to see which one can get to the other side without yielding. Within the city, the bridge is the only connecting point for the numerous neighborhoods that lie to the extreme eastern and southern urban expansion. Traffic is steady.

Beyond its physical importance, however, the bridge stands out as contested terrain in the popular geography of the neighborhood. The railing sides display the territorial graffiti markings of the Roman numeral XVIII, the eponymous symbol of Belén's branch of the 18th Street Gang. It is a point place for drug transactions and a hangout for gang members, who divide their time between the bridge and the relative safety of the tall grasses that line the banks of the ravine. Because it is the sole link between two sides of the city, gang members from other neighborhoods and rival gangs pass through the middle of Belén when they ride public buses or drive by on bikes. Because of the possibility of such incursions, members of the local gang clique must prove that Belén is theirs by representing the gang at this strategic point.

Not all the young men who spend time at the bridge are looking for drugs or flashing gang signs, even if this is the image that most residents conjure up when talking about what goes on there. Its neighborhood position on the main thoroughfare makes it an ideal place at which to meet and hang out. The bridge and surrounding areas are vantage points from which to see neighborhood action.

Figure 2. The bridge, ravine, and Catholic church in Colonia Belén. Photograph by author.

Early on a Friday evening in January 2002, two young men sat on the railing, talking in the low light. Both lived relatively close to the bridge, in different sectors of the colonia. The pair were good friends and met frequently to chat and pass the time and escape the dreary conditions of their crowded homes.

The lone lamppost was in its perpetual state with the lightbulb shattered. In the semidarkness, the youths enjoyed the settling quiet. A small gray Nissan pickup crawled across the bridge, heading west. It gave no indication that there would be trouble. Because of the road's potholed condition, few cars speed, and the pickup was no exception. This time, however, the passenger side window rolled down, exposing the barrel of a .38. The unidentified man inside the cab fired multiple shots. The first hit one young man in the forehead, a shot that should have killed him instantly. The other young man, seeing his friend shot, turned to dive over the railing and into the relative safety of the ravine below.

A bullet caught him in the spine, in the lower lumbar region, paralyzing him from the waist down.

Not waiting to see if they had finished the job, the killers in the truck sped off down the dirt road toward the highway, leaving clouds of dust in their wake.

Community members repeatedly warned me that it was unsafe to hang around the bridge, especially at night. In my conversations with young men and women about community safety, they would identify the bridge and the ravine that it crosses as the most dangerous place in the neighborhood. I had difficulty reconciling this with the fact that the majority of the stories of violence I was collecting occurred elsewhere— in front of people's houses or on specific street corners. In fact, no single place in the community seemed to have more acts of violence associated with it than any other. All places were equally prone to being a setting for violence. However, because of these shootings, the bridge regained preeminence in neighborhood talk of danger. During the weeks after the shootings, the bridge became the point of departure for discussions about youth and violence among people of the community, especially members of the Catholic and Pentecostal churches.

The impact of violence on the lives of neighborhood youth marks locales such as the bridge in Colonia Belén with signature meanings. In this chapter, I explore the contested meanings of neighborhood spaces to demonstrate that such debates stand in for discussions about the moral quality of youth. Youth navigate and negotiate the meanings of such neighborhood spaces through experience and narrative. Via individual experiences, they develop knowledge about community locations, a familiarity they make public and collective through narration and practice. By identifying such neighborhood locations as dangerous, local youth use their history of social relations in these places as cautionary tales to inform their friends about personal safety in these areas. Talk about violent places that circulates among youth not only serves as a warning to others but also generates proxy experiences. Much like Caldeira's (2000) "talk of crime," the stories about the dangers of certain community locales manage fear even as they place such fears in wider circulation. While such talk of violence is generative, it also localizes insecurity in attempts to tame violence. In other words, stories about violent places reduce the recognition of the randomness of violence in

the neighborhood but also propagate fears about neighborhood violence. When youth exchange stories about violence in their neighborhood, they recontextualize the acts, bringing it into the immediate space
of the narration. By talking about violence, youth momentarily have
some control over its effects.

Youth are not the only ones who talk about violent locales in the
community. Almost all locals recognize the bridge within the neighborhood's landscape of fear (Tuan 1979). As such, it is used as a metaphor
both for the disruption of life caused by violent crime and for the moral
corruption of youth. Consequently, both gang and church institutions
co-opt and attempt to redeploy definitions of neighborhood space for
their own uses. Representing themselves through the practice of graffiti
on and near the bridge, local members of the 18th Street Gang marked
the bridge out as their own. Graffiti concretized gang social relations
and made their presence visible to all who traversed this busy thoroughfare. After the drive-by shooting, both Pentecostal and Catholic churches
almost simultaneously sought to redefine the bridge's meaning for the
community. These churches' attempts relied more on rhetorical strategies to transform the history of the place than on efforts to actually
transform the kinds of social relations that took place there. Young men
and women were not fooled by these attempts. They understood that
dangerous places such as the bridge relate more to the contingency of
social relations than to the reputation of the place. In this way, gang and
non-gang youth understood that the valence of neighborhood space has
much more to do with who spends time there and what one does there
than with one-off events that showcase attempts to reclaim parts of the
neighborhood. Youth understood violence to be a product of social relationships that occur in particular places, and not a consequence of the
places themselves.

Youth and the Social Production of
Neighborhood Space

Youth perceived Colonia Belén as being safer than other violent communities, even as they acknowledged that violence and crime occurred
in their neighborhood. When pressed to explain their different attitudes
about their own neighborhood versus others, youth replied with a simple
"porque ya la conozco" (because I know the colonia). Knowledge of their
neighborhood brought personal security through familiarity. During

my general discussions with youth about community safety, I became frustrated by this answer and their unwillingness to comment in greater detail. Yet they often told spontaneous stories about dangerous places in the neighborhood, triggered either by a recent event in these locations or by a similar event elsewhere.

When it came time to conduct formal interviews, however, I decided that one way to approach the subject of neighborhood safety was to have youth draw neighborhood maps, locating those places they saw as most important. As they explained the maps, I asked about personal safety in relation to neighborhood spaces. Their responses echoed the types of stories I overheard in spontaneous conversations. With the map exercise and in overheard conversations youth discursively organized the community around themes of safety and danger. In essence, their narrations create a type of cognitive map of the community's safe and dangerous places. As Merry concludes in her study of neighborhood safety in the United States, "These maps are subjective representations imposed on the physical realities of space and time, distortions of reality that reflect the individual's past experience and knowledge ... [that] guide movements through the [neighborhood] and behavior towards strangers" (1981:172). Talk about violence is a defining feature of the neighborhood landscape, one that youth use to organize their relationship to the community. As we shall see, fixing danger in specific places is a strategy used to diminish uncertainty in the neighborhood as a whole (see Massey 1994:166–172).

Anxious Places: Specific Points on the Landscape of Fear

Stories concerning the violent histories of local landmarks circulated within the neighborhood. These landmarks, therefore, serve as reminders of the most violent types of social relations: homicides, assaults, rapes, and thefts. Many of these places had similar environmental characteristics. In general, they were poorly lit, away from houses, and on the edge of the neighborhood, or they were located on or near major points of traffic, which increased the flow of strangers into the neighborhood. In those places where two or more of these factors converge, the perceived level of violence also increases. Nowhere is this more evident than in the neighborhood's preoccupation with the bridge and its surrounding areas.

When asked to draw his map, Marcos highlighted features of the neighborhood landscape in his description of the dangerous places in Belén:

MARCOS: They say that there at the bridge is a dangerous spot, at the bridge and here on the outskirts where our parish hall is, where we meet. Well, there coming in front of the pool hall there is another dangerous zone.

JON: And why the bridge?

MARCOS: For the reason that there, you know how it's dark and there's a lot of car traffic and there they've always, they've screwed with people, they've wounded them with gunshots and everything. For this reason it's the most dangerous place because it's really uninhabited, there's no light and everything there is ugly.

JON: And why is this main street dangerous?

MARCOS: I say because, for me, this main street is dangerous because, let's say in this main street are people from other neighborhoods. Let's say that this is section one [of Belén], this is Roosevelt neighborhood, and they come from there, the gangs, and how the only place to have fun is in this street because, let's say, this pool hall is there, and this other pool hall is there, and this bar is there, a cantina. So many of these kinds of businesses. So what's going to happen? These people meet there and it's dangerous there because, at times, they sit on a corner [next to the bridge] and there they are messing with people, asking that you give them money and everything. For this reason. And, you know, it's at the edge of the ravine [*quebrada*], and the ravine is a refuge for these thieves, this edge is bad.

JON: They hang out at the edge [of the ravine]?

MARCOS: Yes, because, let's say that they have a problem or do something bad, let's say an assault or they wound another young man, another kid, they just run for the ravine. Like this is the ravine here, and the other side is already another section, section two [of the neighborhood], right? Well, from there they disappear and aren't found. For this reason the edge of the ravine is dangerous.

Marcos's comment reflects common knowledge about dangerous areas in the neighborhood. In his justification of labeling the bridge and the ravine as dangerous places, Marcos identifies environmental characteristics of both. Yet, for Marcos, the types of people and acts that are associated with places are just as important as the natural or built environment.

Marcos understands these social spaces in light of the interplay among environmental factors, knowledge about social relations, and personal experience. Such talk about places is not created ex nihilo. The circulation of discourse on the relative merits and safety of the bridge and ravine originates with the experiences of such places by a few local youth. Talk about one's own, and other peoples', experiences with locales like the bridge affirms for all in the community the types of social relations that occur there. Such stories cultivate a particular attachment to, or orientation toward, these spaces. Stories told about spectacularly violent events in such locales imbue these places with their reputations. Primacy is given to experience; environmental features are drawn upon but are not what makes the bridge and the ravine dangerous.

Martín makes clear that his relationship to the bridge is based on the experience of social relations there. In the following comment, he isolates a problematic relationship with Arturo, a well-known gang member, as the source of an uneasy relationship with neighborhood places, particularly the bridge.

> MARTÍN: Gang members are seen there, gang members that smoke marijuana there at the edge of the ravine, where it's section one [of Belén], ... well, I told you I'm afraid of the pool halls and, let me see, also I'm afraid of a side there in a section of Belén, there by the church, but in these streets here, here by the bridge where they shot those young men, you know the one that died. You were at the wake, remember? I'm afraid of those as well, because it's believed that for this young man they have killed many, a notorious one, Arturo. I don't know if you know him.
>
> JON: Um-hum.
>
> MARTÍN: That's one bad dude. Well, I fear walking over there, close, because I saw how once they shot at him and almost killed him. Well, I also fear talking with him, of finding myself with him there, because suddenly they'll kill me instead of him.

It is not so much that Martín fears Arturo. In fact, Martín and others would assure me that Arturo is a threat only because he has a big mouth and thinks he's tough. What Martín is afraid of, however, is being confused *for* Arturo by being in the places where Arturo is known to spend time. Martín goes as far as to say that most of the gun violence that has occurred on and around the bridge is in fact due to outsiders looking for Arturo. The two young men who recently were shot at the bridge,

Martín tells me, may have been mistaken for Arturo. Social relations among youth are mediated by places in the neighborhood, which in turn become imprinted or tainted by the reputations of the people who spend time there. Martín does not fear that Arturo would do him harm, but rather he worries that by being associated with Arturo, he will be killed. Martín fears becoming a stand-in for Arturo, just as Arturo is an embodied representation of community violence. Place and person become metonymic in Martín's final description, as Arturo stands in for the bridge and vice versa: "I fear talking with him, finding myself with him there, because suddenly they'll kill me instead of him."

When I interviewed Arturo about his relationship with community places, he drew a map that delineated what he called "hot" and "cold" places, with "hot" places being those locations that see the most violence and the most action, and cold places those locations that are calmest (see also Riaño-Alcalá 2002:293–295). The bridge, he says, is one such "hot" place:

ARTURO: We visit Belén's bridge—a special place, a place worthy of death, worthy of massacres, and worthy of violence—this is Belén's bridge. A place that is never going to have a solution and never will. If I were to tell the history of what has happened to me at this bridge, we wouldn't finish now. The tape would run out, and we'd need another and another and another, and that's how it'd be. So that's not even the beginning. Yes, what happened to my carnal, that wasn't much compared to what they have done to me on this bridge. To me, thank God, I've never been hit, their bullets have never hit me, but yes, they've tried to do a little bit of everything to me. So the bridge is way too hot.

JON: Can you give me an example?

ARTURO: An example? You're coming at three in the morning, I'll put it to you this way. You come at three in the morning, you come walking calmly. The police appear. They search you. They don't find anything. They leave you there, you stop because you say, "Dang, they let me go free." In a short while comes a black car, a red car, or whichever car. They stop and go at you with gunshots. They go to shoot you. They shoot a, they shoot a mini-Uzi, a nine-millimeter or a .357, but you give thanks to God because you are below the bridge and not a single shot hits you. This is an example of what happened to me. A miracle saved me and what more can I say?

As if to increase the immediacy of the bridge's relationship to violence, when I ask Arturo to give an example of his own history there, he instead tells a more general story. This agglomerated account of his and others' past experiences parallels the account of the drive-by shooting at the beginning of the chapter. Arturo uses the second-person informal case to place me (and, subsequently, you the reader) as the protagonist in his story. His reading of the bridge as a violent place is made mine (and yours) in the process; a sort of everyman is created so that Arturo's history could belong to anyone. Of course, this is just one example, one of the many he insinuates, and Arturo still maintains overall interpretive authority as the one with the deepest and most violent history.

Arturo illustrates a dangerous attachment to the bridge by giving it a timeless quality that fixes the meaning as violent: the bridge has always been violent and always will be. To make his point timely, he puts his relationship to the bridge in relation to the recent shooting of his carnal by stating that what happened to his carnal (and the carnal's subsequent death) is minor when compared to what has happened to him over the years at that same location. By comparing the death of his carnal with his past history with the bridge, Arturo perhaps exaggerates his own experiences with gun violence. Yet, when compared to Martín's assessment of him, Arturo readily accepts that he is a nexus for violence, because he claims to be the most frequent target. He also places into relief just how lucky he has been to escape the multiple attempts made on his life.

When I later talk with Sergio, a recent ex–gang member of Arturo's gang, he corroborates Arturo's everyman account as an actual occurrence. When I recorded the interview, Sergio had initiated leaving the gang by becoming a Pentecostal less than a month before the interview (see chapter 5). He tells how the gang sent him to execute Arturo, who had decided to leave the gang without authorization. Sergio had mixed feelings about having to kill Arturo, not because of any great affection between the two of them, but rather because he was sent to kill someone from his same gang. Sergio, like other young men and women in gangs, was caught in a catch-22: either kill your gang associates for their wrongs or be killed yourself.

SERGIO: The day came when they gave a mission about Arturo, that I had to kill Arturo. Well, that day came and I was frightened. I didn't know what to do. I went with El Duende and another that they call Vampiro and Títere, the one they killed, did you know about that?

We went. We tricked Arturo, [telling him] that we were going for a meeting, having a meeting there in the orange grove. I almost never spent time with them then. I only spent time alone, only taking drugs. And killing Arturo, well, I was trying to go clean. I was coming clean of what I'd done in the past. So we take him with us, when we're going almost in the middle of the ravine. I remember that I'm taking out the *chimba*'s pipe to point it at him, and Arturo crouches down and says, "No man, wait," he says. "Something fell," he said, and he starts looking for it below there in the darkness. Then, he leaves running, right, like he felt it then, like it wasn't his day. I felt really happy, because what's the use then? I already didn't want to live the same life, because if I were to have killed him that day, the blame would have been mine, because I went to call on his house. That's what they would have said.

This attempt on Arturo's life was unsuccessful, and Sergio was spared having to make another attempt, because Arturo ultimately reconciled with the gang. Yet such accounts add mystique and an aura of danger to places in the neighborhood such as the bridge and the ravine. These types of stories circulate as gossip at the time of the occurrence of violence, and much later, after the fact, as a way to explain the bad reputations of such neighborhood areas. They thus help construct and communicate a common experience of violence in the community that cuts across age, gender, and institutional affiliation (religious or gang).

To some degree such stories are moral warnings about places, warnings that aim to constrict and direct movement in the neighborhood. To be seen in such places metonymically associates young men with those who normally hang out there, according to these stories—gang members, drug addicts, and the general juvenile delinquent (*delincuente*). In a nearly tautological feedback loop, talk about violent social relations and events imprints a sense of danger upon the places where they occur, which in turn creates more talk and implicates all who are seen at such places. Such public spaces become truncated in the process: to spend time in the open at such places is harmful to one's reputation and possibly to one's physical well-being. Fear of violence makes these prominent and public landmarks fraught with ambiguity. The bridge and ravine are unavoidable features of the neighborhood, since people must cross both to reach the other side of the colonia. Yet the violence associated with these places means that using them, especially at night, increases anxiety, which in turn leads to fear about the people one might encounter in these locales.

The young men quoted above all share a common understanding of the bridge as dangerous, an understanding built upon the types of people they know to hang out there and the types of activities known to occur there. Arturo's and Sergio's understanding of place comes from firsthand experience. For them, the bridge is a social space animated by firsthand knowledge of past events that have occurred there, as well as the types of violent encounters they have participated in as near-victim and perpetrator. Marcos and Martín, on the other hand, do not share this immediate knowledge of the bridge; their understanding is mediated through accounts that circulate within the community of young men. But their definition of the bridge as a place also relies on an extrapolation of the kinds of social relations that can take place there. Marcos is aware of whom he could encounter, and Martín fears for whom others could mistake him. The bridge is not dangerous because of environmental factors, but because of young men's firsthand and proxy experiences of the bridge.

Conflict over Meaning of Urban Places in Latin America

While youth gave consistent readings as to the danger surrounding the bridge, church and gang institutions within the neighborhood contested these meanings, each trying to claim (or reclaim) the bridge as their own. The meaning of a place often generates debate. Conflicts over use of space in urban areas and conflicts relating to social relations in particular spaces are also conflicts about meanings of places (Rodman 1993:137). Nowhere is this more evident in urban life than in the contestation over the uses of public spaces and the meanings associated with them. Battles over public spaces, especially highly visible public spaces, are also concerned with social visibility, on the one hand, and erasure or secrecy on the other.

This conflict between visibility and erasure is particularly acute in many Latin American cities. Following a long period of nondemocratic rule, many new social movements in the region have made claims to public space as a way of gaining political visibility.[1] These claims often center on specific architectural forms, such as plazas and parks, or other significant locations within a city, which have long histories as political places where conversations with and about power occur.[2] College youth in San Pedro Sula's public university, for example, occupied the campus commons and registrar's building at the start of both semesters while I conducted research, protesting the byzantine registration process and unavailability of classes needed to graduate in a timely fashion. They camped out for days until classes were made available, putting pressure on the national government for greater funding. Political life also literally takes to the streets in the form of public marches and demonstrations, some of which occur on a regular basis, such as the annual teachers' union and nurses' union marches through the streets of Tegucigalpa and San Pedro Sula, making visible their presence to a forgetful legislature. More recently, the 2009 street protests for and against ousted President Zelaya throughout the country are evidence of the way visibility and appropriation of space work in tandem to demonstrate political will.

Yet contestations over the quality of a particular place and its use need not memorialize a place or be coordinated in its efforts. Such responses, like city or neighborhood beautification projects, can be part of a larger project with "nonpolitical" justification but have political consequences. Attempts by various church groups in Colonia Belén to organize a coordinated effort to clean up the ravine, for example, often resulted in having to coordinate with local politicians to arrange for the transport of trash or the donations for supplies. Political party patronage meant the project would get done, but the patron would also take responsibility for it. There were also neighborhood politics that had to be negotiated, as dumping in the ravine was a common practice for those families who could not afford—or would not pay for—trash removal themselves. Neighborhood cleaning of the ravine set in motion simultaneous debates among locals: the city was abdicating its responsibility, parties were politicking for votes, and some neighbors were taking greater responsibility than others for local affairs. Debates about the ravine, then, were often debates about who had responsibility.

It is not merely the use of public space that is at issue. What people do in particular places in the city becomes metaphoric for political ideologies, among other beliefs. The idea of a sense of place becomes the rhetorical vehicle that refines these debates, distilling the debates into poignant markers of losses or gains in public visibility. In other words, conflict over public space is also always conflict about something else, something more abstract that manifests itself through struggles over places.

Nowhere is this struggle for space better illustrated than in gang graffiti. Although gangs use graffiti to mark the neighborhood as part of their territory, its use extends beyond that of territorial marker. Gang members like Arturo and Sergio possess firsthand experience with violence. However, the gang also perpetuates violence by making its presence known through graffiti around the neighborhood. By doing so, the gang as institution marks public space for the community while also reinforcing individual members' attachment to where they live.

The Social Production of Space through Gang Graffiti

Gang graffiti is a prime example of how the chaotic nature of one's urban environment is controlled through creating specific points of attachment via written symbols (cf. de Certeau 1984:117). Spaces become imbued with meaning due to people's affective and cultural attachments to it (Low 1992; Low and Altman 1992; Rotenberg 1993:viii). Marking neighborhood walls with sprayed graffiti tags is a way for gangs to "represent," or make themselves visible within the geography of the city (Phillips 1999). Writing the names of the gang, clique, and members is more than just staking territory; it is one of the ways that gang members coalesce around a shared identity. As such, graffiti involves making the neighborhood "a place where gang members feel comfortable while also enhancing their survival in hostile circumstances" (ibid. 115). Graffiti transforms an undifferentiated and hostile environment into something of one's own.

Throughout the neighborhood, the stylized script of the 18th Street Gang appears. It can be found on the sides of homes, on the walls around the soccer field, and, of course, on the bridge. The repetitious use of the gang name and the nicknames of its members throughout the neighborhood manifests the social relationships that take place there. As Lefebvre (1991:32) reminds us, social relations alter the physical environment through labor, economic activity, and social interaction. Using graffiti to alter the city is one way in which gangs make themselves known as a powerful urban institution.

Gang members' reinscription of street corners and walls transforms the neighborhood itself as an extension of the group. Indeed, we can see this in the use of the generic term *barrio*, the Spanish word usually used to refer to a neighborhood. For 18th Street Gang members, however, the term is made much more specific; it is used as shorthand for the gang itself.[3] In conversation, gang members rarely refer to their own group with the much more widely used terms *mara* and *pandilla*,[4] instead preferring to use the term *El Barrio*. Witness, for example, how Arturo corrected my confused terminology:

> ARTURO: First of all, those are not maras, those are pandillas.
> JON: What's the difference?
> ARTURO: What's the difference? Simple. Las maras are the MS, they are the mara 13 [Mara Salvatrucha 13]. The 18 gang is not a mara. The 18 gang is a pandilla. Yes, it is a pandilla, what they call El Barrio. Barrio 18 is not a mara like all the rest. This is the difference.

In other words, for gang members, *mara* is used only to describe MS-13–affiliated gangs, while *pandilla* is reserved for 18th Street–affiliated gangs. This distinction is made only when talking about a rival gang— the 18th Street Gang always calls MS-13 mara, and MS-13 always calls the 18th Street Gang a pandilla—but when talking about one's own gang, one's own affiliation, the gang is referred to as El Barrio—the gang—and el barrio—the neighborhood, even though Belén is a colonia (removed from the city center) and not a barrio. In his correction, Arturo designates the neighborhood and the gang as one and the same. In this seamless identification, protecting the neighborhood and representing the gang are equivalent activities, often revolving around the practice of graffiti writing.[5] Writing gang-name graffiti on the walls of the neighborhood expresses a challenge to rival gangs, almost as if in a duel (cf. Cintron 1997:173). By writing the 18th Street Gang throughout the neighborhood, members are throwing the gauntlet, provoking their rivals and expressing pride in the place they call home and the group they call their own. If no one rises to the challenge by crossing out the gang name with another, respect for his or her gang is self-evident. Any challenge to their graffiti causes reprisals in kind. Again, Arturo explains:

> ARTURO: Ok, look, I'm going to tell you something. This is an 18 [Street gang] neighborhood. [A member] of the MS-13 comes here, grabs spray paint and goes at a wall, putting up MS-13, Mara Salvatrucha, and the gang nickname of the guy who wrote it. . . . This is a humiliation for the neighborhood [el barrio], this is to humiliate you in your own house! It's as if you were in your house and I came along and pulled a pistol on you.

Notice again the ambiguity in Arturo's statement through the use of the double signifier *el barrio*. Having some rival gang's name painted on

Figure 3. 18th Street Gang graffiti with gang members' nicknames. Photograph by author.

the neighborhood walls humiliates the community and challenges the gang on its own turf (fig. 3). Arturo makes that clear. Graffiti can be a violent challenge to the sovereignty and respect of the gang.

To envelop the walls and other important landmarks in the neighborhood with the name of the gang is like a protective incantation to ward off the presence of rivals with the prominent position of one's own name. The power is in the naming, in clearly and unambiguously delineating one's own presence (Cintron 1997:176). The lists of names advertise to others who can be found within the barrio, both as the neighborhood and as a social institution. As such, the repetitious graffiti invoke the relationships that make up the space around them. It is as if to say, here, at this corner, or here at this bridge, we are present and ready. Gang members' attachment to their neighborhood cannot exist without these already realized social relationships acted out in space and reaffirmed through graffiti. Every time they walk through the streets, gang members are reminded of where they belong.

Appropriation of Space by Church Institutions

While the gang as institution uses graffiti to proclaim its presence and identification with the neighborhood, churches contest this identification through attempts to reclaim public space. In response to the double drive-by shooting and subsequent death of one of the victims, religious institutions in the neighborhood tried two different approaches to reclaiming the bridge as part of their neighborhood and to cleanse the violent aura that had developed around the landmark. Both the Catholic church and a local Pentecostal church, in keeping with their institutional styles and orientation to the community, used the attacks at the bridge as a point of interest in their ongoing conversation in the neighborhood and the nation over the state of youth.[6] Their differing orientations to the bridge as an index of youth violence reflect their respective orientations toward young men in general. Through the churches' attempts to appropriate and redeploy the bridge as a metaphor, we gain a clearer picture of the successes and failures of these institutions in designing alternatives to youth violence.

Fieldnotes, February 26, 2002. The Rosales' white goose works as good as any dog. No matter how stealthily I try to approach their house, she honks in clear sharp tones that someone is closing in. But this evening no one can hear her bellicose cries as I arrived for my interview with Delfina. On the other side of the bridge, one of the Pentecostal churches performs an evangelizing campaign and their amps bleed out static. Mixed with the white noise were the unmistakable sounds of an electric piano, complete with artificial drumbeats and syncopated cymbal crashes.

I finally caught Delfina's eye through the open front door. "What a racket!" she bemoaned, indicating the general direction of the campaign with an index finger. I had to agree, as the din was loud and off-key. What the singing congregation lacked in musical talent they made up in enthusiasm.

I told Delfina I couldn't interview her tonight: there was too much background noise. She was not too disappointed, and when I told her I was going to check out the campaign she laughed at me, saying, "Careful Jon, you might convert!"

Despite still being early in the evening, the street was quiet, with few people out. As I rounded the corner and came to the bridge, the hoarse screech of the pastor's voice greeted me.

"Satan is the one who is taking bodies, is killing out there. He carries his chimba and shoots people."

This hushed the small crowd and, I must admit, gave me pause as I stepped out onto the bridge. After the dramatic silence the pastor continued in her urgent tone, "But when Jehovah says, 'Enough!' this chimba of Satan's no longer exists.

"I have been preaching here in Belén for six years. Six years I have been here. I know of at least six youths who have been killed here in Belén at the bridge in the six years I have been here. . . . We have disastrous things going wrong with youth. We need more youth here so that we don't bury any more youth in the cemetery. The only one who can defend us is God, not any pistol."

I reached the outer edge of the small crowd, guided by the pastor's voice. I couldn't shake the sense that she had it wrong, that perhaps we were all guilty of violence by association, no matter what our position in the neighborhood. When is Jehovah going to say "enough"?

The pastor seamlessly blended the end of her sermon into the final prayer session. Young and old alike raised their hands skyward, their heterogeneous and cacophonous voices exhorting forgiveness from God. The pastor continued to scream into the microphone, demanding that the young men of Belén come forward and confess their faith in Jesus. After minutes of this fervent display, only two young women climbed onto the stage, awaiting the pastor's hands on their heads to cleanse them of their sins. No young men heeded the pastor's urgency. Why, I wondered, was this campaign so unsuccessful when I had seen other evangelizing campaigns in which whole groups of gang members had turned themselves over to the custody of the church?

Fieldnotes, April 1, 2002. Early on Good Friday morning, I waited in the churchyard with a growing number of Catholics for the Vía Crucis, or procession of the cross, to begin. The light blue stucco of the church building merged with the brilliance of the clear blue sky. It was going to be a hot day. People arrived from all over the parish, some in hired buses and others in the overfilled beds of volunteered pickup trucks. Belén's church was where the procession would start as it wound its way through the poorer neighborhoods, stopping at the other three churches in the parish along the way. The Vía Crucis reenacts the stations of the cross, from the time when Jesus was condemned to death, through the public ridicule, his execution on the cross, and his burial in the tomb.

Figure 4. The second station of the cross for the Good Friday procession. Photograph by author.

Unlike the triumph of Palm Sunday's march through El Progreso the week before, the Vía Crucis was a somber event shared by members of the neighborhood churches.

The sun was strong by the time we began to push out of the church-yard's metal gates and onto the dusty streets. Two young men from Belén's youth group led the way. They carried a simple four-foot-by-four-foot, heavy wooden cross. Two large nails stuck out where Jesus' hands would have been, a much subtler reminder of the crucifixion than the representations of Jesus dying on the cross.

Once on the street, we slowly walked across the bridge, spreading out until there was no space for cars to pass around us. Marking the second stage of the cross, a small wooden table covered with a white cloth, offset slightly from the main road, sat on the west side of the bridge. On the makeshift altar there were two white candles flanked by glass vases filled with purple plastic daisies, and an eight-by-ten framed illustration of Jesus receiving the cross from Roman soldiers (fig. 4). In the picture,

Jesus was on his knees, doubled over by the weight of the burden. Bearing the cross is a powerful Catholic metaphor for the sacrifice of Jesus' death and the burdens of the sins of the world, which he assumed when accepting death. Taking the cross also represents the sacrifices Catholics make for their faith.

We stood in a horseshoe around the table. Carlos and Tavo, both stone-faced, positioned themselves to the left of the table, facing the crowd with the cross. Tavo led us in prayer, petitioning God for the end of violence in Honduras and the world. "O God, we ask that the murder and injury of youth in our country end." Tavo's voice was unsteady, as if tired from the weight of carrying the cross even the short distance from the church.

"We beg you, O Lord, hear our prayer," the crowd replied in a subdued, collective voice. Before we marched on up the street toward the other stations of the cross, Carlos led us in a Lord's Prayer and a Hail Mary to seal our submitted petitions.

The scene presented an emotional juxtaposition. We prayed for the end of violence, especially youth violence, near the bridge, still tainted by the recent shootings. The two young men holding the representational cross metaphorically asked a mute and haunting question: Is violence the cross the young men must bear?

Memorialization and Solidified Meaning

The Pentecostal and the Catholic churches employed similar approaches to the bridge as neighborhood place. Although they acknowledged that the bridge was a prominent site for violence in the community, they chose to crystallize the meaning of violence in that locale by making ad hoc memorials out of the bridge, thus reinforcing the gang's interpretation of its importance. This is clearly evident in the Catholic church's use of the bridge as a stop along the Vía Crucis. A committee of church elders had opted to make the bridge a stop in the procession. Setting up a temporary altar on the site just a few months after the shooting episode was a public way for the church to acknowledge youth violence in the neighborhood. The young men carrying the cross presented an interesting tableau in which young men, through carrying the cross, became emblematic victims, much as Jesus was a victim of the malice of the crowd. Unknowingly, perhaps, they were living memorials for the young men killed on that spot, because they represented all past victims of violence.

The Pentecostal church's use of the bridge as the site for a multinight evangelizing campaign was also an attempt to memorialize the bridge, capitalizing on its notoriety. Unlike the Catholic church, which set up a physical, albeit temporary memorial, the Pentecostal church used the space of the bridge as a living, momentary memorial by enacting the campaign on that spot. The pastor invoked the memory of the bridge's past through her sermon, calling on the young people to repent in the present. Through the rhetoric of her sermon, she created a connection between the bridge and the cemetery, both memorials for the dead. The obverse that one must assume through this connection is that only through coming to the church will young men find life.

Transforming the bridge into a momentary memorial may seem in agreement with the ways that young men and women understood the bridge in their narration of acts of violence that took place there. The churches present a picture of the bridge as being inherently dangerous because of what took place there and because of who was present. In adding the bridge as a stop on the Via Crucis, the Catholic church reinforced the association between violence and young men, demonstrating that violent death is the cross that young men must bear while social and political factors remain that maintain this association. The Pentecostal church, congruent with its general emphasis on the importance of individual salvation, attempted to transform the bridge by converting young men to the power of the church. Both approaches proved unsuccessful, for, as Arturo reminded me, the bridge will always be a violent place because the gang marks it as such.

By memorializing the bridge, the Catholic and Pentecostal churches attempted to draw on the metaphorical value of the landmark. The two churches' intent lay somewhere between spontaneous and planned memorial. By using the bridge as a momentary memorial, they sought to solidify its meaning as a violent place. Community members of both churches obviously felt they were tapping into a common expression of sorrow over youth violence by using the bridge as a metaphor for the memory of the dead. Yet by crystallizing meaning in the place of the bridge, they ignored something that youth know well enough: violence is not easily localized or contained. By using the bridge as a metaphorical device, the churches wanted to trap meaning in place, without taking the wider view. Though violence may occur in various places, the dynamics of interpersonal interactions are exacerbated in a particular space.

The churches' responses cannot change the reality of youth violence, because the violence will continue or move elsewhere until the conflict between rival gangs and the conflict between gangs and the nation-state ends. The act of temporarily memorializing the bridge was nothing more than a token gesture. If the churches had wanted a more intervention-ist approach to ending violence, they could have chosen to clean up the ravine, cut the grass along the edges, improve the lighting around the bridge, paint over graffiti, or implement community watch programs. Their memorials reinforced the general understanding in the neighbor-hood that the bridge is where violence occurs and, as such, should be off-limits to any decent young man or woman who values their reputa-tion and life. Memorializing the bridge as a violent place only dimin-ished the public space available to neighborhood youth.

Diminishing Public Spaces

I do not wish to suggest that young men and women in Colonia Belén or elsewhere in El Progreso live in abject fear, unwilling to ever leave their houses because of the threat of violence. If anything, the contrary is true: young men and women are, for the most part, surprisingly mobile, traversing their neighborhood streets, socializing, spending time on street corners, going to play pool, going to and from school and work. The generalized fear of violence from outside forces, a fear that could be overwhelming and paralyzing, in fact is managed and diminished in the process of associating violence with particular places or people. Although places like the bridge rightly do have reputations for violence, of the many stories about neighborhood violence and the violent acts that occurred while I was living in Belén, just as many happened on resi-dential streets in front of houses. There was very little pattern to where violence actually occurred. As a strategy, using talk about violence to fix fear in specific locations is successful precisely because it is mostly talk about social relations and a comment on the violence done to one's reputation. In a way, young men and women put fear in its place by locating violence in other people. This placates their anxieties, thereby shunting violence away from their most immediate surroundings. To hang out at the bridge is socially damaging to young men's reputations, and potentially physically damaging as well because of social proximity. Yet, as Massey points out, "it is not proximity in itself which is unset-tling but also the nature of the social relations, and most particularly in

their aspect of power relations, of which proximity is the geography"
(1994:167).

Intimate knowledge of the community, born of interactions with its
denizens and participation in the rhythms of daily life, helps map social
space. The rhythm may have changed over time as more pernicious
forms of violence have become increasingly widespread for youth, but
the quality of the interactions is still based on experience. It is through
interactions with others that understandings of places, even understandings of violent events, are produced and circulated. Intimate knowledge
is the engine that generates information about violence. Intimate experience of place instructs and constructs both the social and the physical
reality of urban life (Rodman 1993:137).

All such considerations bear heavily on the use and availability of public space in working-class and working-poor neighborhoods in Honduras.
Such neighborhoods never have had a proliferation of public spaces;
there are no public parks, rarely even a soccer field. What they do have,
however, is an active street life; sitting in front of one's house on a hot
summer evening talking with friends and neighbors is a favorite pas-
time. Young men hang out on street corners to get a better view of
the street, to see people passing by, to gain a bit of distance from their
families. Street violence, therefore, critically impinges on the quality of
the only public space available; it severely strains and wounds sociability. Architectural transformations, such as the walled houses of the
middle and upper classes (Caldeira 2000), or modernist city planning
that eliminates pedestrian access to city life (Holston 1989) need not
be present to signal the death of the street. Indeed, death of the street
can just as easily—and much more dramatically—be caused by death
in the street.

If both Low (2000) and Caldeira (2000) are correct in asserting the
ideological and practical connection between open and free public space
and democratic political institutions, their conclusions hold much weight
for those subjects who are denied access to public space. It has become
increasingly dangerous for young men in Honduras to lay a claim to
public spaces in their communities of residence. The violent politics of
territoriality instituted by gangs create generalized anxiety about being
in public, and thus undermine sociability. Diminishing public spaces
for youth presage the elimination of public visibility for youth, particularly as working-class and working-poor young men are demonized as
perpetrators of violence in the media and the popular imagination of

the nation. Their moral exclusion from public life coincides with their forced exclusion from public space (cf. Ruddick 1998).

Moral exclusion from public life for poor young Hondurans is increasingly the general rule, as youth are no longer at risk, but are "*the risk* . . . as people out of place and excess populations to be eliminated" (Stephens 1995b:13; emphasis original). In other words, it is not just that youth put themselves at risk by hanging out at the bridge, but that youth at the bridge are a risk for all others in the community. The high rate of youth violent death in Honduras gives numerical expression to this process. Moral exclusion from public spaces and the public sphere fuels youth violence as it excludes youth from opportunities for advancement and personal development or even the ability to voice opposition to prevailing policies. The protests by university students were well contained within the walls of the institution—they were not visible to a wider public. In part, this was because "moral" youth are not found in the streets. Only *delincuentes,* or delinquents, roam the avenues of the city or are found on street corners, or so the logic goes. Youth are to be neither seen nor heard, unless within the protective space of sanctioned institutions like the church.

3
Thick as Blood
Street Ties, Gang Tattoos, and Graffiti

The Cemetery

Few sights are sadder than an unkempt cemetery. I stood just inside the entrance to El Progreso's municipal cemetery with Manuel and Lucas, staring in disbelief at the disorder in front of us. When I had asked my two perennially out-of-work young friends to help me count headstones, looking for some way to gauge the youth death rate in the municipality, I thought that their odd looks meant disapproval of my macabre request. But now, looking out at the overgrown vegetation and dilapidated cinder-block tombs, I realized their looks were more about the state of the cemetery.

There was no evident logic to the placement of graves, no Arlington-like rows. Instead, there was only a jumble of tombs, cast like lots. Wealthier, established families tried to maintain the ancestral crypts, erecting wrought-iron fences with locked gates that mimic their houses. Other families, if they could afford it, placed the coffins in aboveground cement tombs, some beautified with glazed tile and built-in vases. Many of the graves, however, looked like they had been forgotten, with mortar crumbling in the humid air and plots surrendered to the vines, grasses, and tree roots. The very poor buried their dead underground with no cement overlay and only a wooden cross to mark their place. There were many graves without markers. Names and dates were less important than the memory of where a friend or family member was buried.

Counting tombs was overly optimistic of me. I turned to my assistants, about to tell them I didn't know where to begin and maybe we should abandon the idea, when Manuel said to me, "Sergio's family is buried near the back wall. I remember where. Do you want to see it?" I had heard from many of my friends about Sergio's family, how both his parents had died of AIDS complications and that his older brother had been shot down outside his home by rival gang members. It wasn't until after his parents and brother died that Sergio became heavily involved in the gang and started smoking marijuana and crack.

Manuel seemed eager to show me, so I told him, "Sure, if you know where it is, let's go." The three of us took off down the narrow path that wove its way through the front half of the cemetery. After only ten minutes, the path disappeared. Manuel and Lucas climbed on one of the tombs and jumped from top to top. I am not a very superstitious man, but I hesitated nonetheless, feeling the impropriety of skipping from grave to grave. Lucas looked back to make sure I was following and told me to hurry up. "Don't worry," he laughed. "It's only the dead we know that bother us." The vegetation choked the stones. I couldn't see the ground, just variations of greens. There was no other way to continue. Setting aside my uneasiness I followed Lucas and Manuel, hopscotching across the cemetery.

We stopped near one of the larger crypts. Painted pink, the stone lintel bore the surname of the current mayor. It too had seen better days, with chipped paint, a cement finial broken off at the upper corner, and the bars of the entrance's gate bowed where someone had tried to break in. Nearby was a wide tamarind tree, which shaded us from the late-morning sun. By this time, I was sweaty and wishing I had brought some water.

"El Títere is buried over there." Lucas jutted his lower lip to point toward a blue-tiled tomb.

Manuel shook his head in agreement. "Oh yeah, over there."

"The blue one?" I asked, unsure whether such an elaborate tomb would be erected for a notorious gang member.

"No," Lucas replied, moving in the direction he indicated. "The one next to it."

We approached the plot, standing on the slick surface of the adjacent blue tiles. El Títere's grave was plain and anonymous, except that someone had tagged the top with the ornate Roman numerals XVIII in orange.

"There's no name," I said, stating the obvious, as if the gang tag were not identification enough. "How do you know it's El Títere's?"

"I went to his interment," Manuel replied. "I like to go so I remember where the families bury them."

Lucas and Manuel started trading names of other young men buried in the cemetery and argued about their locations. Some of the names were familiar to me, like El Títere and Tico; they were names of young men I never met, but whose memory circulated in the stories my friends told. After about ten names, Manuel and Lucas stopped their litany.

We were close to the back wall. I could hear the murmurings of traffic on the other side. Manuel pointed in the distance. "Sergio's family is over there. We're close." So off we went again, hopping. Lucas called to me, "It's the tall one there."

We approached a triple-decker grave. "His brother's on bottom," Manuel informed us. "Then his dad and then his mom. It's cheaper this way. You don't pay for more land." It also keeps the family together, I thought.

"See?" Manuel reached out with his left hand to touch the tomb where thick orange lettering dripped down the side, the same color orange as the "XVIII" on Títere's tomb. It was the epitaph Sergio placed on his family's graves. "I came with Sergio when he did that," Manuel told us. "See there, it says, 'My dear family, I will always love you.'"

Sergio's biography of personal loss, uncontrollable anger springing from abandonment and grief, and the tragedy of seeing over half his family die is, unfortunately, typical of many of the gang members I met. I had heard others in the neighborhood talk of how Sergio and his brother, Julio, had been left orphaned in their early teens. The two brothers took divergent paths after that defining moment. Julio joined a Pentecostal church, and Sergio became a central figure in the local clique of the 18th Street Gang. While neither young man ever voiced it in such terms, it was evident from their actions that they had turned to these two community institutions for not just emotional but economic support. Although they had been left with their parents' house, at ages fourteen and fifteen, neither boy was prepared for what it meant to live on their own. Several years had passed by the time I got to know both young men. Julio, at age nineteen, appeared well adjusted, integrated into the community life of his church and working at a local maquila. He regularly ate at the homes of church members, confided in them, and drew strength from his lengthy prayer sessions. Sergio's trajectory proved to have different results. Often withdrawn, fighting a growing crack addiction, and increasingly despondent as to what the future could possibly hold for him, Sergio was also struggling with increasing disillusionment with regard to the five years he had spent in the 18th Street Gang. Although he looked back fondly at the initial few years and the support and escape the gang provided, it was the past year or two that began to make Sergio question his life. Numerous members of his gang cohort had been murdered, including his closest friend, Títere. In many ways, it was the death of Títere that brought an additional crisis upon Sergio's life. He had suffered the loss of his parents and now was living through the additional loss of someone he considered his brother, more so than even his biological brother, Julio.

Sergio's story encapsulates the process of street socialization outlined in the seminal works of Diego Vigil (1988, 2002). Vigil outlines the very processes that lead young men like Sergio to seek refuge and support from gangs. Although the specific circumstances at play in Sergio's life may differ from those of Vigil's Chicano Angelino informants and may be more tragic, the concomitant forces guiding identity formation and marginalization from mainstream cultural and economic resources are quite similar. While Vigil has rightly pointed out the psychic and social impact of street socialization, the mechanisms of this transformation and socialization have been largely ignored in favor of exploring the macro forces of social marginalization. I offer here a more detailed view of how this micro transformation takes place, of how youths like Sergio lose access to non-gang support, allowing the gang to subsume their individual and social identities through the entextualization and incarnation of gang values. As an explanatory framework for the social transformation of neighborhood youths into 18th Street Gang members, I turn to de Certeau's account of the way social groups exert influence.

In his discussion on scriptural economies, de Certeau highlights the ways in which social groups initiate individuals into the advent of new relationships through submitting the individual body to social writing techniques. At times metaphoric, the use of "writing" for de Certeau encompasses the forces social groups exert on an individual to manifest norms and laws and to subject individuals to the social order. He sees any bodily transformation as representative of these forces—from shaving one's legs to wearing makeup. The transformation, then, is how individual, embodied flesh becomes entextualized as the vehicle for social laws while these laws simultaneously become incarnate in the individual.

While his formulations are intentionally abstract, de Certeau's insistent use of "flesh" for the individual and the techniques of writing for the social group highlight the literal ways in which gangs in Honduras enculturate individual bodies into members of a corporate entity through various writing techniques of their own. First, intimate pair-bonding relationships between gang members are cast in fictive kin terms. Gang members call these relationships *carnal,* most often glossed as "blood brother."

Yet the literal definition from the Spanish—"flesh"—provocatively distinguishes the visceral nature of these relationships. Likewise, tattooing and graffiti take the blank, unsoiled spaces of the carnal body and neighborhood territory and imprint a new identity, transforming both by christening them with new names. "Give me your body and I will give you meaning. I will make you a name and a word in my discourse," de Certeau claims, mimicking the persuasive voice of sociality (1984:172). In what follows, I explore this relationship of naming and writing with the literal "flesh" of gang members and the metaphoric skin of the neighborhood—its walls—to demonstrate the transformation that gangs require of their members and the multiple processes through which this occurs. Gangs, more so than the Catholic or Pentecostal churches in the neighborhood, require a near total identification with the corporate whole. I turn first to explore Vigil's idea of street socialization and the formation of *carnal* relationships more fully through the lives of some of the active and ex–gang members I knew.

Street Socialization and *Carnal* Relationships

Vigil (1988) formulates that given the relative weakening of families, the peer group on the street socializes boys on how to become men. Survival for these youth depends upon understanding the ways of interacting with others on the streets. For gangs the peer group supplants traditional kin networks, replacing much of the emotional and material support they might have received in the household. Javier, one of the founders of the El Progreso, Honduras, branch of the 18th Street Gang, illustrates perfectly Vigil's explanatory schema in describing to me the move from his childhood home to the gang:

> JAVIER: I had a really complicated childhood, because, Jon, my mother got with another man [not Javier's father]. This, this is not the same, it's not the same as truly being with your own parents. She would go wherever he told her to go, do whatever he told her to do. He would always punish me a lot, me and my brother he would punish us a lot. He would punish us and so we never had a peaceful life until finally, when I was thirteen years old, I had to leave the house. Yes, and this was when I found a refuge in the street. Yes, I pretty much became a lost gang member there in the [neighborhood]. I became the 18th [Street Gang].

Feeling insecure and uncomfortable in his mother's household, Javier eventually left to join the welcoming environment of the gang. In many respects, the gang as peer group competes with the natal household and kin group. If the family is where "normal" socialization is to take place, young men like Javier who are gradually pushed out of the family, or those like Sergio, whose family is diminished through tragedy, find that the street and peer groups step in to continue the enculturation process. In fact, gangs utilize kinship terms and model their organization after familiar ties to teach street values to new recruits and incorporate them into the corporate identity. Javier continued to describe what he calls the "brainwashing" that occurs within the gang:

> JAVIER: Well, first, [the gang] brainwashes you, telling you what they do, saying various things like, "We are a family, we are a family and we support those that don't have family," and that "we give you food although you don't work," and that "if there is a problem for one of us, it's a problem for all of us" . . . and that "here no one fails because we are one single family." And they go on brainwashing you and brainwashing you so much that they tell you, "Here no one is going to prohibit how you dress," . . . they say, "Here you are going to look your best, you are going to get earrings and get tattoos, and we aren't going to charge you anything," they say. This is how they start to brainswash you.

In Javier's description, the gang replaces many of the primary functions of the family, providing food, shelter, and protection, yet within a space that, unlike parental authority, allows young men the freedom to dress and behave the ways they want, in countercultural fashion complete with symbols of gang affiliation, such as the use of earrings and tattoos. Indeed, the gang's insistence on certain fashions such as wearing oversized clothes and having earrings in both ears is the first instance of de Certeau's transformation, where the new recruit comes to alter his appearance and in so doing takes on the corporate, family-like values of the gang. The support of the gang is expressed through the sharing of a style, while the value of freedom from mainstream social norms manifests in that same countercultural style. The trade-off, however, is that the freedom to dress in a certain way is itself submitting to a new subcultural norm. Javier's comments indicate the insistent juxtaposition gangs make with family life, holding up for members and new recruits this idea that, while kids may come from less-than-ideal home situations, the gang will stand in as the perfect image of a supportive family.

Despite the tendency to formulate the peer group as a replacement for familiar care, most street peer groups are rife with physical violence and abuse. Indeed, hierarchy and power are forcefully enacted, causing distrust and breeding animosity among peers. To reinforce the loyalty to the corporate group in a context of mutual distrust, gangs stress the importance of ritual and fictive kin bonds between individuals. In some instances, gangs institutionalize these bonds through the use of kin terminology that emphasizes both the fraternal relationships and the elective association with the gang. In Chicano, Mexican, and Central American gangs, for example, the supportive nature of the gang as family is strengthened by pair-bonding between gang members. Although the gang may have a corporate structure and even promote itself as family, within the gang the primary relationships develop between blood-brother pairs. Such blood-brother bonds, known as *carnal*, are mentoring relationships (Vigil 1988:426) and serve to transmit knowledge as well as strengthen loyalty to the group. Strong bonds between youth enhance survival chances in hostile situations, such as in areas where gangs are under threat from others, by creating an element of trust in an otherwise insecure setting (Phillips 1999). Arturo, another 18th Street Gang member from the same community as Javier, describes the difference between "friends" and carnales, or "blood brothers":

ARTURO: I am not very friendly. I have lots of friends but not lots of blood brothers, *friends*. I am going to tell you something, I'm going to enlighten you on something: there are no friends in this world. . . . [Friends] are like saying they're your dogs. I don't have friends. I have a *carnal*.

When I asked how he chose his carnal, Arturo offered this reply:

ARTURO: Good question and good answer. You yourself said the two things: how did you choose him [to be your carnal]. Simple: you choose by hanging out with him, speaking to him, eating with him, walking with him, if it is possible, sleeping in the same room with him. . . . You learn to trust him with your shit and to distrust him too. Then, when you start to trust and distrust him, you understand that life is not a great mystery, but that life is a responsibility. You know that you need someone else, it's not just you [in the gang], it's not just you, there are lots [of us in the gang]. But we don't make [carnales] with lots of them. . . . You know that if you are always in the large

group, the police will kill you. So we are two. Choose your carnal. . . .
Try to choose him, try to select him and try to educate him. He is
going to be faithful to you as much as you are faithful to him.

Members of the same gang, according to Arturo's metaphor, are as
if they were a pack—fellow dogs that could, and often do, turn on each
other if a member has violated some gang norm or law. The carnal, on the
other hand, is the person you choose to support you at all times and on
all the missions and activities the gang might send you out to do (thieving, spraying graffiti, participating in gang warfare). It is the carnal that
has your back. Arturo is clear on this: life in the gang is uncertain, filled
with possibly treachery. One needs a carnal to equalize the distrust and
feel the support of family that the gang promises. If gangs did not offer
this dual structure of "family" and "blood brother," in which blood-
brother relationships create the camaraderie and trust of fictive kinship, it is unlikely that gangs would be as successful in recruiting young
men and women. The gang members I knew and spoke with across El
Progreso's three main gangs (18th Street Gang, MS-13, and Los Vatoslocos) all expressed that it was the camaraderie and support of their fellow
members that they most would like to keep if able to leave the gang.

The gang capitalizes on the strong *carnal* bonds to coerce its members into doing its collective will. When members are sent out to do missions, they are sent with their carnal. Sergio described how this works in
the following hypothetical situation:

SERGIO: Let's put it this way, I get along with you, I get along well
with you. I spend time only with you, just us two. And maybe they
[the gang] tells us, "Look, you two have to go on a mission. You have
to go and do that thing." And that thing they give us eighteen days
to do it. If we don't do it in eighteen days, then we're in for it; that
is, they kill us. And so we go, eh, and in these eighteen days we must
do it, there's no way around it. We have to go together then, and this
they do . . . to see if we are truly carnales. . . . If the two stay alive, you
understand me, it makes one feel great . . . and this is where one is
most hooked then to feel, like I told you, like Superman, powerful.
One feels greater pride, greater valor.

Such "missions," as they are called, collude to reinforce the bond
between carnales while also submitting both young men to the will of the
gang through coercive means. These acts of violence are acts of solidarity,

cementing *carnal* relationships, because they imply complicity and possible danger. The threat of death is doubled, because although a gang member may be able to decide to risk being murdered by his own gang for not completing a mission, he would be less able to risk the life of his carnal. And the more he does for the gang, the more the gang supports and celebrates him, increasing his self-worth.

The sociability that violence engenders between carnales and, by inference, with the corporate gang, is literally a double-edged sword. First, gang members know that if they do not fulfill the "missions," or orders to kill others, given by members of the gang, then they, and possibly their carnales, will be murdered by members of their own gang. Such a consequence entrenches young men involved in gang life even deeper, embedding them in an emotional morass. Gangs, as social institutions, enforce compliance to committing violent acts through the levy of guilt at being the cause of a friend's death, and fear that one might be the next victim. Being a perpetrator of violence extracts a psychic toll on the individual, because of the kill-or-be-killed mentality that gangs foster. Later in his interview, Sergio slipped from the hypothetical case excerpted above, to using an example based on real events to forcefully illustrate his point at the way gangs put its members in a double moral bind.

> SERGIO: The other day, this happened days ago, a friend of ours, he would hang around with us . . . he was from [colonia] Morazán. They called him the Wraith. Listen up! The Wraith they called him. And we killed him, because he raped a gal from his same neighborhood. This has happened as well. Don't you think it is difficult to be a part of this? It is not a game, like they [gang members] say. This is not a game, because one gets involved, they can't leave it. And it can be your carnal, then, listen up! Your carnal, the one you spend time with most. And if he screws up, maybe to you they [others of the gang] say, "You have to kill him. If you don't kill him, we kill you." One has to do it, then, because one doesn't want to die.

Sergio was sent to murder The Wraith, who had raped a young woman from his neighborhood, something most gang members will not tolerate, because they view themselves as the protectors of the neighborhood. To victimize one's own neighbors, especially in unprovoked ways, violates one of the central tenets of gang life. Sergio uses this story to relate to me that gang members must be on call to follow the instructions of the gang, even if these instructions entail murdering your closest gang friends. If you do not follow through on the orders, you risk being the target of murder. Sergio, in his moment of reflection on gang life, wants to assure me that gangs are serious business, not the game that some youth may believe them to be. Gangs are serious because they cause great pain to the individual by placing him in conflictive situations in which a gang member must murder or be murdered. One's need for self-preservation always conditions one's affective ties with others. The threat of violent retribution against one's carnal gives a young man pause as to how his actions might impact someone so close to him. It is this intimacy that is reinforced through the use of the term *carnal*. Carnales are of the same flesh, the same substance. Their bond is no longer as fictive kin. It is as if their identities become fused into one because of the threat of retribution and their shared destiny. They are social Siamese twins. Enculturated through shared histories of violence, gang members lose part of their individual identity in order to gain acceptance and membership within the gang. They submit themselves to the regulatory methods of gang governance.

Members of the 18th Street Gang continually reminded me that, unlike their rival MS-13, there was no "leader" and no strong sense of hierarchy within their group. Again and again I was told that "*todos tenemos la palabra*," "we all have the word," or the ability to speak out and set the group agenda, both within the local clique and at meetings between cliques. *La palabra* refers to the unwritten norms of gang life and the actual written rules and communiqués that arrive with gang members who have traveled between Los Angeles and Honduras.[1] Although there is an ethos of egalitarianism, in reality, there were some members who had greater ability to speak out than others. Respect was given to those who embodied and lived the values of the gang and upheld the written laws inherited directly from Los Angeles, considered to be the most authentic due to LA's reputation as the cradle of the organization. Experience, zealousness, and valor also play into one's ability to claim "the word." "The word," then, is both formal law and accepted practice, referencing a certain scriptural authority couched in a lived, embodied experience. The force of the "the word" as a set of subcultural practices is that it defines the individual through a domestication process that shapes and inscribes the body (de Certeau 1984:165). The literal manifestation of de Certeau's metaphor of cultural inscription is the art of body modification. Eighteenth Street Gang members enact "the word" through the written communiqués the gang traffics: tattooing and graffiti. The collective will is made flesh through these inscriptions and, as the following narrative makes clear, even when marked over, leaves a palimpsest, a residual reminder of the past.

The Mask Remains

Fieldnotes, June 20, 2002. The God Is Love Pentecostal church was a far cry from its evening glory, now in the glare of the midmorning sun. The church, housed in a converted cinder-block home, was shut tight with the windows and doors closed and padlocked. It seemed a sad face, tired and weary as an elderly man, with its sagging walls and drooping tin roof. Construction was set to begin up the street on the new church building, and the parishioners were excited about having a new worship space, something to reflect their perceived position as God's favored people.

A small alleyway, nothing more than the width of a single person, separated the church from the neighboring home. I turned into the cool, shadowed place, my sight temporarily overcome by the change in lighting. I'd never used the side entrance to the church before—heck, I wasn't even sure that the side entrance existed—but the padlocked front of the church was enough to let on that if Sergio and Lucas were still inside, they had to have gotten in through the side door. At the far end of the alleyway, a peeling blue painted door was pressed shut. Upon closer inspection, I could see it was not locked, at least not from the outside. I looked at my watch. Just after 9:30. Sergio and I had to be at the tattoo removal clinic before eleven for another session.

I stood in the shade, contemplating whether I should knock or just go in. Sergio had started joining Lucas in sleeping at the church. Lucas always portrayed it as a public service he was doing for the church. Walter, Lucas, and a couple of other guys from the church would spend their nights sleeping on the smooth cement floor to guard the amplifiers and other electronic equipment from theft. While the other guys would rotate through, Lucas spent almost every night in the building. He wouldn't say it, but I knew he had no real place to go. His uncle's house, across the street from where I lived, was not a welcoming place to stay, as his family would chastise Lucas for not having steady employment. He was no longer a boy, they would say, he needed to take responsibility for his life. Sergio was in an even more desperate position than Lucas. Sergio had no home. His parents were dead and his mother's house had been taken over by an aunt who refused Sergio entrance when his gang involvement and drug habit increased. In fact, most members of his extended family refused to offer him food. In the short time since Sergio decided to convert, the church had become his uneasy support system, providing shelter and at least one meal a day given by some of his closest supporters in the church. I, too, had become part of Sergio's support system, whether I realized the full extent of what that meant or not.

Today was to be our third week of treatments at the tattoo removal clinic. I had convinced Sergio that if he were to really demonstrate his desire to leave the gang, the only way for this to happen would be to erase the ink sketches on his body that peeked through his T-shirts. For someone who had been in the gang for as many years as he had been, Sergio had relatively few tattoos—only five—and of those only one proclaimed the gang number eighteen in Roman numerals around his left shoulder. Sergio reluctantly agreed after I took him along on one of my clinic visits. It was a painful process. The tattoo site was injected with a mild analgesic, and then an ultraviolet heat gun would cauterize the skin, obliterating the top dermal layers and the foreign ink. It would take several visits to remove all of the ink from one tattoo. It was a procedure that could cause permanent disfigurement if the burns were not cared for properly. The clinic brought Sergio and me even closer together, as I became charged with accompanying him, getting him to his appointments, caring for his wounds, and listening to his anxieties. I wasn't sure how much more I could take. Why had I agreed to take responsibility for Sergio? When was Sergio going to take responsibility for himself?

I decided on a compromise. I knocked on the door at the same time that I pushed it open. Small rays of sunlight played across the suspended particles of dust in the room, illuminating just enough space for me to see the lumps of two bodies wrapped in blankets on top of pieces of cardboard, insulating the youths from the hardness of the cement floors. I called out as cheerfully as I could: "Hey! It's Jon. We need to get going for the appointment, Sergio. It's 9:30 already."

The lumps twisted and turned and slowly revealed the naked torsos of Lucas and Sergio in the half light. Lucas, forgetting where he was, cursed, "Son of a bitch, Jon. Is it really 9:30?" He shook his head rapidly to awaken. Sergio unwrapped himself completely from the blanket and rolled up to a standing position. His boxer shorts hung loosely from his waist, a few sizes too big for his cracked-out body. He raised his arms over his head, stretching his small frame. The light was just enough for me to see that the bandages had fallen off his shoulder and back. Sensing my eyes upon him, Sergio looked at the left shoulder where the tattooed XVIII had been. He scrunched his nose in disgust. "It's ugly man. It's gonna scar." He moved his right hand to the wound and turned his torso toward me, as if beckoning me to have a look. Moving from the door-frame I walked to where he and Lucas slept. He was right; the wound was puffy and looked infected. Sergio hadn't been caring for it.

"It's that way because you need to keep it covered. If you want the skin to look good, you need to protect the wound and keep it clean." Sergio mumbled something in response and grabbed his jeans from a nearby plastic lawn chair. "Besides," I added, defending the whole process, "the nurse said it would take several treatments to remove all the ink."

Sergio faced me while he pulled on his jeans and tightened his belt. Standing shirtless, he examined the rest of his torso with his eyes and left hand. He was sullen today. His hand moved up to his chest, to where his last intact tattoo remained, a picture of a clown mask, a toothless smile of comedy. "I'm done, Jon," he spoke into his body, but I could hear him plainly enough. "I'm done. I'll finish the rest of the process on the others, but the mask stays." Still looking at the blue-black ink lines on his dark skin, he repeated as if for emphasis, "*Se queda la máscara.*" The mask remains.

Sergio's ambivalence toward removing the tattooed evidence of his gang membership is best understood in the context of his interpersonal relationships and recent past. While I helped out at the tattoo removal clinic, I met many young men whose tattoos were far more problematic, in terms of placement and design, than Sergio's (fig. 5). His five tattoos consisted of: one set of gang numbers, three small points at the nexus of his thumb and index finger, a botched portrait of a Lempira Indian on his right arm, a spiderweb radiating out from his elbow, indicating time served in jail, and the comedy mask on his chest. The mask, in particular, was different from his other, more amateur, tattoos. It evinced careful, bold lines and an almost artful sensibility. It was crafted, not just some gang trademark.

The higher quality of the tattoo, however, was not the sole reason for Sergio's reluctance to remove it from his body. The tattoo was etched on his skin by Títere, Sergio's closest friend, and his carnal. With Títere's murder several months before, Sergio was holding on to a portable memorial of his best friend. Evidence of Títere could be found throughout the neighborhood. Spray-painted tombstones bearing his name tagged

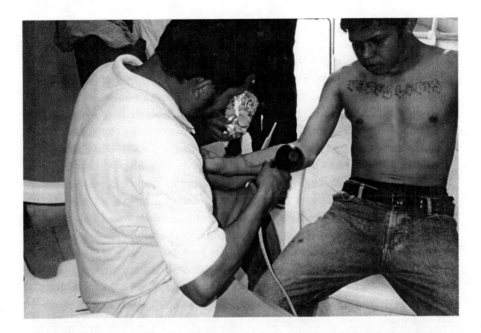

Figure 5. A young man from the Los Vatoslocos gang getting his tattoos removed. Photograph by author.

several walled memorials, a product of Sergio and fellow gang members' attempts to remember their dead. At the community soccer field, straddling the border between two neighborhoods, however, was another vibrant reminder for Sergio of Títere. Sprayed on almost six feet high and the whole width of the field was "Eighteenth Street Gang," written in a form of Gothic script. Two artful masks, comedy and tragedy, flanked the moniker. The comedy mask, with its slanted eyes and round nose with the number eighteen inscribed inside, was done in the same style, the same hand even, as Sergio's tattoo. Títere had been the artist for both.

The boundary between self and society is neatly expressed in the membrane of the skin, especially when that skin has been inscribed through the process of tattooing. From Terrence Turner's (1980) exploration of the importance of the skin as the vehicle through which social ties are expressed and constitutive of the social self to Alfred Gell's (1993) monumental synthesis of the role of tattooing in precontact Polynesia, the ethnographic and theoretical literature on body inscription highlights exterior social imposition on the individual interior. Gell's detailed analysis, in particular, demonstrates that hierarchy, status, kinship, and age affiliation—all social states of being—subject, tame, and in some cases enculturate the individual through the process of tattooing. A tattoo, for Gell, "is always a registration of an external social milieu, because it is only in relation to that milieu that the tattoo has meaning" (1993:37). The social group powerfully—and painfully—exerts its presence into and under the literal skin of the individual tattooed body. The tattooed individual will never be registered the same.

Sergio's tattoos were also part and parcel of the society in which he lived, and it informed their social significance, the web of relations threaded through the ink on his skin. Bearing visible tattoos in Honduras is a dangerous enterprise, as the popular conception—largely borne out through experience—is that only gang members defile their bodies in such a way. Media images of heavily tattooed gang members flood the television news reports and newsprint stories to such a degree that even middle- and upper-class youth who have fashionable tattoos done on trips to Miami or Houston are careful not to place them on readily visible parts of the body. Even though the contrast is great between a well-placed "tribal"-style tattoo on the upper shoulder and the Gothic lettering of MS-13 splayed across the chest or face, any tattoo can place the owner in danger. Due to the rise in gang activity and the moral panic associated with all things gang-related, Honduran police and military patrols use the presence of tattoos as cause enough to detain a young man and question his allegiance.

Closer to Sergio's own life, however, his tattoos, as with other gang members, literally registered him as a member of the 18th Street Gang. It is through the act of tattooing that the gang possesses its members. In his discussion of body markings among the Waiwai, Mentore (2005), drawing on Gell's work, concludes that tattooing is a process of revelation, revealing the inside (the psyche, the ego) on the exterior of the body for all world to see. Tattooing, in this formulation, exposes the inner workings, desires, and essence of the tattooed individual. While I do not disagree that this may be the case, especially for elective, decorative tattoos, gang tattoos work in the opposite direction as well, so that there is an internalization of the exterior world by the gang member who becomes tattooed. That is to say, the tattooed gang member literally gets the gang under his skin, pierced into the core of his being, marking his identity with the larger gang territory and the group ethos.

This shift in state of being for gang members is partially a product of the conditions under which tattoos are aggregated and inscribed on their bodies. While I was volunteering at the tattoo removal clinic in El Progreso, the young men who came to remove the written evidence of their gang membership shared similar stories as to the histories of their tattoos. I would look in amazement at the variety of delicate places these young men would have covered with ink. The placement went well beyond the mundane arm or chest tattoo. Gang names, Gothic-script numbers, and Roman numerals would show up across the kidneys, on elbows, the napes of necks, and, unbelievable for me, on the cheeks and across the forehead and brow ridges. Facial tattoos were agonizing to remove, even with the use of local anesthetic. My initial inquiries as to how one gets his face tattooed would receive the same set of answers: they were drunk or high at the time, so jacked-up on crack or blissed-out on marijuana that they didn't feel the pain of having the soft tissue on the face punctured with the homemade needle apparatus. More than a few young men described the process as one of betrayal by their fellow gang members, stating that they had passed out and, upon awaking, found their faces tattooed.

Once the brand of ownership by the gang is placed in such a visible location on the body, there is no going back, no strategic hiding of their identity as MS-13 or 18th Street Gang members. The branding revealed to the greater public exactly who the young man belonged to for all time, effectively sealing his exclusion from mainstream society (see Gell 1993:27).[2] Tattoos, however, are just one of a set of signifying practices that allows a member to represent their gang affiliation and which encircles the member in webs of allegiance (Conquergood 1994). In essence, tattooing is but one form of inscription and, as such, references other forms through its iconic similarities. Most importantly, tattooing is intimately tied to the use of graffiti. Indeed, what is a tattoo but graffiti on the flesh?

Other Forms of Naming: Graffiti and *Apodos*

In her extensive study of gang graffiti in Los Angeles, Susan Phillips highlights the importance of communication through writing and gesture as a form of boundary maintenance between gangs. While this may sound elementary—that graffiti on neighborhood walls mark territorial boundaries—her point is not that boundaries are fixed, immutable entities, but rather that the process of representing the gang continuously creates, maintains, and contests boundaries and allegiances between gangs and within a particular gang. Ultimately, belonging to a gang is "about representing what you love and actively creating it in the process. . . . It shows your homeboys and your enemies who you are and what you stand for" (Phillips 1999:117). Because representing occurs in public space, it is easy for uninformed outsiders to think that gangs "claim" neighborhood space through the use of graffiti. In all actuality, there is little proprietary interest and few claims of ownership on the part of the gang. Rather, neighborhood spaces become the billboards for gangs to advertise their presence to others in the neighborhood.

In Colonia Belén, as elsewhere throughout the north coast of Honduras, there were some forms of graffiti more visible than others. Quickly sprayed tags, or *placas*, of "Calle 18," "18th Street Gang," or the number eighteen in Arabic or Roman numerals, while lacking in artistry, were prominent features along heavily trafficked corridors, especially the two main streets that bifurcated the neighborhood. These tags let others know they were about to enter the presence of 18th Street gang members, and that they should act with sufficient respect. At times, the placas acted as warnings not only to members from rival gangs, but also to motorists and pedestrians having to use the common corridor for their commute. Gang members would occasionally set up makeshift tollbooths, charging non–Colonia Belén residents to traverse the bridge. They would target taxis and, when particularly emboldened, buses, that would stop at the bridge to let passengers off. The placas were supposed to communicate to all moving through the area that the 18th Street Gang was there, representing (and, in gang members' view, protecting) the area from incursion.

Yet, perhaps more instructive, at least for the relationship between individual members and the gang as a collective identity, is to examine two types of graffiti in which the individual is memorialized. While tags scrawl out the name of the gang, what Phillips calls "roll call" graffiti list the names of active members at the time of the graffiti. These lists mark a presence in the community, too, but instead of the corporate identity, it provides the altered identities of its individual members, through the exclusive use of gang *apodos* (nicknames). The use of the *apodo* is crucial, because it demonstrates the process of change—a baptism of sorts—into the gang. Apodos are given out of love, marking a young man as part of a network of affiliation to those in his clique (Phillips

1999; Vigil 1988). While innovation can sometimes occur, most apodos are recycled, borrowed from members in other cliques and, more significantly, brought to Honduras from Los Angeles, so that one's apodo is specific to the subculture. Most often, these names are English loanwords transformed into something more Spanish: El Black, El Brown, Casper/Gasper, Joker, Puppet/Pupet, Ghoul/Goul, Lightning/Litenin. A young man given such a name may himself be unaware of what the meaning is. Sergio, Arturo, and others would ask me to provide glosses in Spanish for their names and the names of their fellow gang members. In some cases, due to a member's similarity in appearance or style with another, apodos can be handed down, especially in the case of a name of a fallen gang member. This was the case of a much-loved gang member, El Monfy, a name which carried on to several generations, so that roll-call tags enumerated Monfy 2 and Monfy 3 from the original. Apodos are names that are granted to new recruits to signify their altered state. Most often, they are given by one's carnal. The elicitation of the name in conversation and through roll-call graffiti refers back to the origin of the name, the one who named you. You are not just El Black. You are El Black because your carnal gave you that name.

The intimacy of names and their repetition in graffiti may indicate a certain narcissism on the part of gang members, a way of seeing their names in lights, as it were. Yet names written on street corners and across the bare walls do more than satisfy the ego. Under the script of the gang and names, roll-call graffiti list the individual apodos of present, active members. This provides a visual reinforcement of the idea that the gang is a collective made of individual members who are themselves tied through historic relationships. And because in the poorer neighborhoods of El Progreso graffiti is never removed and rarely painted over, the names remain even if the individual listed is no longer alive (fig. 6). Sometimes a post hoc addition will be seen next to the name of a fallen comrade, placing, in English, the letters "R.I.P." Sergio, after Títere was gunned down, found every instance of Títere's name and added the memorial. He also added Títere's tomb to the memorial graffiti tombstones sprayed on a couple of the more-protected walls in the neighborhood. Then, as if to remind everyone who Títere had been in life, the same day he lettered his parents' tomb with the graffiti epitaph he also tagged Títere's tomb with the Roman numerals XVIII.

Naming—the use of given apodos, the repetition of those nicknames through graffiti, and the recursive use of the gang name in tattoos—binds

Figure 6. Tombstone graffiti of the 18th Street Gang. Photograph by author.

the individual to the corporate group. The gang calls to its members, "Give me your body and I will give you meaning. I will make you a name and a word in my discourse" (de Certeau 1984:172). Street socialization in gangs is this very naming process, a repetitive, circular use of words to encircle a young man and make him part of the collective enunciation of gang identity. The tattooed skin and the graffitied wall are both points of representing the individual's role in maintaining the group. The writing, though, is performed primarily by the individual through the person of the carnal. The flesh of his flesh, his blood brother, is cementing the relationship, doing the signing of the gang's name to inscribe a young man into the interpretive whole.

Conclusion

Fieldnotes, March 29, 2002. It was one of those typical hot afternoons in the dry season when the sky is a searing blue clear of clouds. The dust from the unpaved roads had become unbearable and caked the crevices of my sweating white body. Behind the knees, in the crux of my elbows and at the corners of my eyes, fine lines of brownish-red traced over these vulnerable spots. I'd been walking through the neighborhood with Sergio for over an hour, taking photographs of graffiti. He was a willing guide, as the walls and their history interested him as much as they did me. Street corners with lists of names and the quick tagged XVIII all had a story that Sergio knew. Not a braggart, he would say matter-of-factly if the graffiti was from his hand.

The endpoint of our tour, however, was the soccer field bordering the main thoroughfare of the neighborhood. In the local geography of gangs, it was not the safest of spots from rival defilement, but it was a highly visible location. The road marked the far edge of 18th Street territory for the time being. The world of MS-13 started just a few blocks away. The graffiti along the side and back cinder-block walls bordering the soccer field were a point of pride for the local clique—oversized letters with gothic flair in the serifs, a collection of tombstones arranged in a pyramid dedicated to the fallen, and two different pairs of the comedy and tragedy masks showing that while we live we must laugh and cry. It was the most impressive example of graffiti I've seen. I may have been underwhelmed by the style at other points on Sergio's tour, but here, this was what my exposure to films about gangs had made me come to expect. I passed by the soccer field almost daily, but this was the first time I got a glance at the names.

We walked parallel to the wall at just enough distance to see both the detail and the composite picture. Sergio pointed to the tombstones. "See, we added those names recently. Títere and Shadow. Take a picture," Sergio directed my camera. "See, Títere. You know who Títere was?"

I nodded vaguely, although I did not know, really, who any of these gang members were. I was still associating apodos with given names and, with no person to associate it with, I would get confused as to who was who. Sergio pointed down the wall to the more intricate pair of masks and said, "See those? Títere did those. He did all the writing. He could do it. It was his talent." Whenever the gang wanted style, wanted to really represent, they'd call on Títere to do the graffiti. As if to add emphasis, Sergio unbuttoned his short-sleeved shirt, revealing the thin cotton band of a white A-shirt. Peeking out from behind the white gauzy material were two upward slopes of ink just darker than his skin. Sergio pulled the undershirt aside to reveal an identical comedy mask as the one on the wall. "See," he said, "Títere did this one too. He was my carnal. Just him and me from the beginning." That was all he'd say on the subject.

I made some lame comment about how good the tattoo looks, how it resembled the graffiti. Sergio nodded again as he buttoned up his shirt. I still didn't know who Títere was. It would be another month before I would make the connection between the young man I saw sprawled dead on the street six months before with the artist and friend Sergio described.

Sergio's simple act of opening his shirt, pointing to the tattoo and the graffiti images, and naming the artist of both graphically illustrates the links between gang inscription practices and the enduring bonds of friendship, even unto death. These links are visceral for Sergio; they have become a permanent part of who he is, literally part of his new social skin since joining the gang. While Sergio's story may be exemplary of the kind of relationships among tattooing, graffiti, and friendship I am suggesting here, I do not think it is unique. Perhaps the difference is in degree, and not in kind. Any connection between a young man and his gang is one worked out through the flesh, be it in blood-brother relationships, tattoos, or wall writing. The concept of flesh, of blood ties, is not merely metaphoric for a substitute family. Relationships to and through the body are what constitute those very same relationships. The individual body is the channel through which those relationships flow.

Graffiti and tattoos orient the gang member's body spatially within the realm of the neighborhood and conceptually within the social boundaries of the gang. The iconic similarity between the name sprayed on the wall and that same name etched on the skin is the immediate, visceral recognition that you belong. Your carnal is the author of these markers of your social and psychological identity as a gang member. Through him, your relationship with the gang is entextualized—the social rules, your identity, your future is all written out, enveloping the body like a protective sheath of social relationships. At the same time you become the exemplar, the embodied law, the gang made incarnate through the visual stance and body markings engraved upon you. It is this near-literal process of entextualization and incarnation that is the root of street socialization, a continual etching of the laws on the gang member's body coupled with the willing incorporation of the subcultural style and demeanor that gives him strength, purpose, and support in a world where he had little. Because it is worked into the flesh, symbolized through the term *carnal*, these new relationships are difficult to sever and come with a blood price.

Sergio's link may no longer have been so strong with the institution of the 18th Street Gang, per se, but the memory of his carnal was something he did not want to lose. Points in the neighborhood geography elicited Títere's memory. The mask on his chest did the same. Sergio was trapped in the semiotic reference. Unwilling to remove the tangible evidence of Títere's life and a vestige of his former life, he would ultimately fail at unbinding himself from the web of allegiances, obligations, and names that is the gang. My efforts to lead him to disfigure his tattoos were naive and uninformed. In the moment, in the heat of trying to support a conflicted young man who had become my friend, I may have done violence to his body equal to that of the members of his gang. I didn't fully understand the internal upheaval, the emotional and social struggle Sergio faced in trying to leave the gang for a "new life" as a Pentecostal. To erase Títere's tattoo from his body would have been the ultimate act of betrayal by Sergio to the memory of his dead friend. In his mind, nothing could replace that bond: no one else in his old gang, not some gringo anthropologist, not the supportive members of his church, not even the God he began to pray to for forgiveness. No one could equal the support and love Sergio felt from his carnal.

4
The Making of Community and the Work of Faith

"We Live as a Community, Not as Individuals"

Doña Eugenia is a frail-looking, spindle-thin woman, but spying her through the open door of her humble house, roughly kneading dough for flour tortillas, I didn't doubt her strength. It was the inaugural meeting of Colonia Belén's Catholic *comunidad de base* (base ecclesiastical community, or CEB), and I could think of no better place for it to be held than doña Eugenia's house. She and her daughters are active in the church's women's group. Her family also embodies many of the prototypical characteristics of CEB families: female-headed household, poor but not destitute, and a family emphasis on the importance of education. All three of her daughters have finished high school, no small feat when many of their contemporaries (mid-twenties) haven't finished primary school.

On this August evening, the last month of my field research, about twenty participants sat in a large circle on an assortment of white plastic lawn chairs and long wooden benches borrowed from the church. Knowing how active the youth of the church are, it came as no surprise to me that almost half of the participants that night were also regulars of the youth group. I sat down next to Martín, who immediately disengaged himself from conversation with the older woman sitting next to him to elbow me in the ribs slightly. I tipped my head toward his. "Look who's come," Martín said quietly, jutting his lips out slightly to point in the direction across from us and to the left. Through the smoke and dim light, I made out the figure of Arturo and two of his gang buddies. I knew from previous conversations with Arturo that he converted to Pentecostalism for a brief spell, ultimately returning to the gang. I never expected to see him and his friends at a Catholic event. I couldn't figure out why they were here—if someone had invited them, or if they found out about it from neighbors. Arturo caught me looking in his direction and nodded his head upward, chin thrust out in that silent greeting that indicates respect and intimidation simultaneously.

After the opening prayer, the facilitator of the evening, Chago, who is also the facilitator of the youth group, welcomed everyone and invited them to listen to the evening's gospel reading. Meetings were organized around a central New Testament reading that was used as the focus of discussion to better understand the meaning of faith and the words of Jesus and the apostles. The meaning of the passage is supposed to develop organically from the ensuing discussion. Chago, in a voice that matched his robust body, read from Matthew 15:10–11, a passage that describes Jesus' "heresy" against the Pharisees. When asked why Jesus' followers did not follow Jewish food taboos, Jesus proclaimed that it was not what went into the mouth that made a person unclean, but rather what went out of a person's mouth that made the person unclean. Or, as I understood it in Spanish: *La mancha del hombre que sale de él* ("a man's mark or stain is what comes out of him").

There was a moment of reflection before Chago asked us to go around in the circle to comment on the passage. The first person to his left was José Luis, a young man of twenty who had been struggling with his marijuana addiction and trying to leave the 18th Street gang. This had led him on a religious odyssey, it seemed, because I had seen him days before at a Pentecostal small-group meeting. Later in the week, after he had made a formal conversion to Pentecostalism, he would tell me how hollow he had felt, how he had been feeling dead inside. He looked troubled as he prepared to speak, his compact, muscular body tightly wound as he sat upright and severe in the plastic chair. "Instead of expecting God to change you," he spoke in a quiet voice to the group, "you have to be ready to change for God. All this time I have been wanting to change, it is true, but I was expecting God to do it for me. But that's not it—it's not just wanting to change, not just the desire, it's that we have to have the will as well, and without the will we can't meet God."

He paused, as if knowing that what he just said didn't quite fit with the Gospel passage, and then continued as if to answer the verse from Matthew more directly. "From the heart," José Luis said, tapping his chest with his fist, "comes the war, the struggle. In my case, to change how I was before, I have to change my heart to change the violence in the community because from there [the heart] comes one's feelings (*sentimientos*)."

Replying to what José Luis said, Arturo looked directly at José Luis, then at me, and finally at Chago's face: "You change for yourself, not for the community. Ha! Why would you want to change for the community when it should come from your own desire?"

Chago, never afraid to speak his mind, met Arturo's gaze and replied, "No, the community is a part of the decision as well. The error that many fall into is that they say, 'The change is only for me, me, me.' Our most important prayer says 'Our Father,' not 'My Father.' We live as a community, not as individuals."

Chago turned to look at José Luis, saying, "We do things and think that all of the community is going to reject us. All the problems that youth have fallen into, who is responsible for them? They themselves, not the community. They judge themselves thinking they can't return to community life."

Chago's mother-in-law echoed his statement: "In a tragedy the community is always there—they don't judge, no matter what you may have done. There are no bad youth, there are only people who say that they can't change."

Chago, still replying to Arturo, continued, "Conscience can be a cancer that eats away at us, because God knows even our very inner thoughts. Even thinking of wanting to shoot another person—only the thought, of wishing someone dead—these thoughts do us harm as well. Other people judge everyone else's lives, when only God has the right to judge." I could tell by the look on Arturo's face that he did not like the way the talk was going, that he did not agree with Chago and the others. He shook his head from side to side. His eyes glowered with hostility from across the circle. He and his two friends left almost immediately after we had said the final prayer. As Martín and I walked back to the street where I lived, it dawned on me why Arturo may have been there. The house Chago rents and the home of Arturo's aunt, where Arturo has his room, abut each other. Chago's outdoor sink faces Arturo's backyard. They are neighbors.

The above account explores the tensions between changing oneself and the role of one's community in the transformation of antisocial behavior. The interaction among Chago, Arturo, and José Luis provides three perspectives on the issue of youth violence and community. José Luis speaks from a position of wanting to change his life. He connects the desire to change with the will of the individual to end community violence. Without willpower, he cannot change himself. Arturo interprets José Luis's comment in a way José Luis perhaps did not intend. Arturo believes that José Luis draws a connection between willpower and the role of the community in exerting pressure to change one's behavior.

Arturo does not want help from anyone. He feels the community inter-feres in other people's business without understanding the dynamics of, in this case, gang life. He emphasizes a disconnect between community sentiment and the behavior of young men like himself. Chago, however, indicates that José Luis is partially right and that Arturo's negative view of community assistance stems from his stubbornness. Chago wants it understood that the Catholic approach to community is inclusive of everyone, including gang members, and that only through the support of the community, of everyone working together, will violence end in their neighborhood. Discussions at CEB and other church meetings circulate ideas about what it means to be Catholic, both within the church and in the neighborhood. Catholic group meetings modeled after CEBs pro-vide a forum for reflection on faith and the practice of one's faith. Just as the meeting ended without resolution, and indeed seemed ambiguous as to the role of both the individual and the community, the response of the Catholic Church as an institutional resource for personal reforma-tion/transformation does not offer an easy resolution either.

In this chapter, I explore the rhetorical construction of "community" among Catholic youth as a way to explain the connection between their actions in the neighborhood and their faith in God. Taking Urban's (1996) insight that community building is a discursive enterprise as a point of departure, I examine the ways in which participants in Colo-nia Belén's Catholic youth group focus on the experiential aspects of *being* a church in their neighborhood through the way they talk about their church participation and belief in God. Derived from a progressive Catholic theology known as "accompaniment," their understanding of a relationship with God parallels their relationship as a community, a relationship that consists of a trust and faith in God and one another. Their approach to youth violence in their neighborhood is to be an inclusive, supportive group who meet violence through cries for com-munity. However, Catholic youth are also ultimately aware that being an inclusive community through accompaniment is an untenable solu-tion to youth violence, because it leaves youth open to the dangers of violence as well. If Catholic youth were to identify in solidarity with all youth, as a theology of accompaniment suggests, they would have to be associated with violent young men. Instead, Catholic youth appro-priate the church's moral narrative of being an inclusive community as an ideal built on forgiveness of others, as well as the ideal of acceptance of others.

Somos un Grupo: Catholic Youth Group

For young men and women in contemporary urban Honduras, the general climate of violence against youth diminishes opportunities to feel a part of community life. Youth in El Progreso find that the Catholic Church offers the most institutional resources for them, especially in the absence of secular NGOs or governmental social programming. In the city, it provides personnel, funds, and organizational cooperation for youth-oriented services. These programs represent a historic commitment to social programming that the Church continues in a wide variety of arenas. Partly because of the social distrust created by gangs, and partly because of violent retribution on the part of state and para-state entities, youth feel disengaged from the communities in which they live. Suspicion and presumptions about young men's and women's amoral and antisocial behavior draws swift divisions based on how youth should participate in their community. In many places, it is best for youths not to be seen or heard from at all. One way for youths to reinsert themselves into community life is by demonstrating to others that they are social and moral beings, not individuals who are bent on harming others.

At the local level of the neighborhood or parish, the Catholic Church engenders community participation by youth through the creation of youth groups based on the CEB model. The Catholic youth group in Colonia Belén was part of a citywide system of youth groups. Some groups were more successful than others in terms of membership and participation. Belén's youth group was unique in its ability to draw a wide spectrum of youth from the neighborhood and differed from other groups in a number of ways. The most obvious differences between Belén's group and others in El Progreso were that Belén's was predominantly male (although with a small strong female core group) and that it attracted many youth who were not active Catholics (meaning that they did not attend Mass on a regular basis). The content and style of each youth group depended upon the church with which it was associated. Some groups criticized others as being nothing more than a social get-together. Members of the youth group in Colonia Belén considered theirs to be highly successful in all areas—membership, participation, and the balance struck between social activities and discussion of social issues. They met twice a week to discuss social or religious issues from a Catholic perspective. These issues ranged from AIDS, to the influence of rock music, to gun violence, to the role of faith in their lives and the meaning of prayer. Teams of two or three group members would present an issue and orient the discussion by including relevant Bible readings, usually from the New Testament. The youth group also orchestrated its own community-action programs by coordinating fund-raising for families in need of medical treatment, collecting food for the poor, and carrying out other community work projects.

As successful as the youth group was, it was not without its conflicts. Discussions could become heated, even if they concerned mundane issues such as what kind of project the group should do next or how the money they collected from their fund-raising efforts should be spent. Group members would raise their voices to be heard over others, and sometimes meetings would erupt into shouting matches between members trying to argue their respective points of view. After one particularly heated meeting, I walked back in the direction of my house with some of the young men of the group.

Fieldnotes, November 7, 2001. The four of us discussed how there seemed to be problems in group cohesion and getting along. Not wanting to discourage them, I said, "Sure, but every group always has some sort of problem at some point." Pepe, who also serves as the representative at parish-wide youth group meetings, replied, "Exactly. You should hear what the other leaders of groups say about their groups. They are by far worse than us."

"So why does our group work so well?"

"It's because they [other groups] don't have the same kind of understanding (*entendimiento*) that we have between ourselves."

The other two shook their heads in agreement. Pepe continued: "When a new member comes to our group we encourage them, talk to them, make them feel welcome like we did tonight with the new guy and we did when you came the first time. Other groups, no, they just leave them there."

Pepe embeds two ideas in his reply about the success of the group. He indicates that the group is a welcoming place, even to first-timers, that the group really tries to be informal and interact with visitors in a way that makes them want to return. Group members also foster a special kind of understanding among themselves. Despite the passionate, sometimes chaotic discussions that occasionally ensued during meetings, there was an understanding among group members about how to interact—that everyone had a right to say their piece. No one seemed afraid to state exactly what he or she thought. Meetings often aired out hidden tensions in the group, and no subject was taboo. When things got out of hand, when tempers or emotions ran high and the group seemed to falter on whether or not it would be able to overcome the current "crisis" because someone had overstepped boundaries, something always pulled the group back together. At these moments, talking to friends about problems in the group, they would inevitably reply with a common refrain: ¿Somos un grupo, verdad? or, "We are a group, right?" Such a reply was akin to saying, "Hey, aren't we a community?" In the face of differences of opinion, group members often brought up the fact that they were a group, as if to highlight their sameness as members. This served as a powerful rhetorical reminder of the community they had created, the friendships that had developed as a result, and the love and obligation they felt toward each other.

Despite their penchant for heated discussions, group members truly conceived of themselves as a circle of friends inserted into the wider neighborhood community. The group brought together young men and women from all over the neighborhood and provided a social outlet, especially in facilitating friendships between young men and women. As well, their involvement with the youth group kept them active as participants in the neighborhood. Their recognition as a self-proclaimed community, through their calls of being a group, provided a positive model for how to relate with others. No matter what differences of opinion arose, no matter how heated the disagreements were, everyone was connected through living as a community. Chago's directive on the importance of young people's association with the community was clear in his statement at the CEB meeting described earlier: "We live as a community, not as individuals." The repetition of this and similar statements highlights the rhetorical importance "community" has for Catholics' approach to guiding youth.

At the Intersection of Morality and Community

Group identity, whether in a kin group or a Catholic youth group, is founded on the common ground of community ties. Members emphasize their similarities to enforce ideals of cooperation and cohesion. As Urban argues for the kin descent group, it is through the circulation of discourse in the form of narratives, myths, and everyday conversation that "groupness" is defined, such that the "discourse encoding of the group as actor—as subject or object—is the crucial feature of group-ness" (1996:146). In other words, what a group is, and what it does, materializes out of narratives about what the group is supposed to be and what it should be doing. The intent is in the discourse as much as in the action. Indeed, discourse binds intent and action together. Thus, when faced with a disagreement, youth attempt to assuage disgruntled attitudes with the cry, "Hey, we are a group!" They reinforce the idea that as a group they must act together and relate to one another with respect, despite disagreements. It is a discursive act that reinforces the idea of what being a group is all about.

Discourse about group identity forges community, builds a common identity, and from this position has social force in the world (Urban 1996:171). It links the group through time and space, giving it conti-nuity, shared origins, and common purpose. It is also discursive acts, through "narrating reality," that inform us of "what must be believed and what must be done" to belong to a particular community (de Certeau 1984:186). In this sense, narration, which creates community, also creates moral imperatives through indirect instruction as to ways of acting in the world. When Durkheim asserted that obligations toward God parallel a group's understanding about members' obligations to one another, he was, in essence, stating that one's relationship to God and one's relation-ship to society are based on the same moral principles (1995:212–215). In a similar way, talk about community is really talk about morality, and vice versa. When members of a community talk about what it means to be a community, they are also talking about moral ways of behaving. For example, at the CEB meeting described above, the moral critique leveled against Arturo and other gang members was that they saw themselves as being separate from the community, and hence not under its moral influence. To view oneself as being outside of community influence is the most immoral position one can have. We also see this in Chago's insis-tence that we pray as a community, that the Lord's Prayer is a collective voice—the "Our Father," and not the singular voice of "My Father"—that petitions God. The collective voice beseeches God for forgiveness, as humans should forgive one another. Chago alludes that, ultimately, we can relate to God only as we relate to one another. Likewise, when Catholic youth group members raise the issue of group identity during heated disagreements, they are also calling on the moral influence of group identity to equalize tensions and bring everyone back within the regulation of the group.

The Catholic Church as a whole has undergone profound institutional changes in Latin America over the past forty years in the way in which it perceives itself as a community and the force of God in the lives of believers. To understand how members of a Catholic youth group in El Progreso approach youth violence in their neighborhood through integration into the community, we must first look at the recent history of the Catholic Church. The ecclesiastical and theological innovations that developed from the doctrinal reforms of the Second Vatican Council (1962–1965) had great impact in Latin America. In Latin America, Vatican II allowed the development of new church models, especially in the face of rapid urbanization (Berryman 1996), secularization (Vásquez 1998), and a steady decrease in church resources (Gill 1998). The Latin American Catholic Church came to understand itself in new ways in relation to the community that it served (Smith 1991:95–97). Catholics in Latin America also conceived of new relations to one another and new ways of relating to God.

The New Catholic Community

Drawing on the Vatican II shift in orientation toward worldly matters, the 1968 Latin American Bishop's Conference (CELAM) in Medellín institutionalized the Latin American church's commitment to social life through declaring a "preferential option for the poor." The church made a radical break with its traditional allies—the political and economic elites—in favor of emphasizing the socioeconomic reality of the bulk of its believers in Latin America. By broadening the scope of its concerns in Latin America, CELAM, in essence, passed judgment on current injustices and demanded a theology of accompaniment with the poor in their struggles.

A preferential option for the poor and a theology of accompaniment required a new relationship between priests and the popular classes. In Latin America, church hierarchy modified ecclesiastical models for the realities of serving as a church among the poor and dispossessed, developing praxis-oriented CEBs (Levine 1994:194–195). Base communities, as an ecclesiastical organization, emphasize horizontal relationships over vertical relationships (Hewitt 1991; Levine 1990; Maciel 1990). This means that, unlike the traditional church's hierarchical chain of command, CEBs value the bottom of the hierarchy ("the people") as the basis of church authenticity (Hewitt 1991:6). For example, at the

CEB meeting described at the beginning of the chapter, there were no religious officials present, and although Chago was the leader of this meeting, at subsequent meetings other members would take over that position. Members were responsible for the running of the meeting and the perpetuation of the group.

In the social science literature, much discussion has centered on the social and political role of CEBs, especially on the ways in which as an institution CEBs reinvigorated a stagnant civil society in times of oppressive dictatorships.[1] Yet just as profoundly, the implementation of CEBs and other forms of Catholic community groups reinforced a new image of God. Cooperatively, as Catholics were forming and practicing CEBs, their attitudes about their relationship with God were changing as well. And new attitudes about God nourish new attitudes toward relating with others in one's community and nation.

For example, in El Salvador, the protracted civil war, years of repressive government violence, and a general climate of social distrust created a situation in which progressive CEBs were one of the few options for expression of community solidarity. Archbishop Romero's *pastoral de acompañamiento* strategy (a pastorate of accompaniment with the poor) stressed the need for the church to be in struggle alongside the people. A theology of accompaniment is part of the ideological cement of the progressive church movement.

Central to theologies of accompaniment is a social definition of sin as alienation from one another. Sin is the reason for social ills such as poverty, oppression, human cruelty, and exploitation (Lehmann 1996:101–103; Smith 1991:34–36). A social definition of sin is the basis for a Christian critique of class inequality and exploitative capitalist development, resulting in a moral-ethical judgment of processes that alienate humans from God and from one another (Lancaster 1988). Base communities work toward liberation from the sin of alienation by bringing communities together for shared reflection on the word of God and by working on collective action to change their immediate surroundings to be more just. Justice through public welfare projects bridges the alienation from others, while reflection on scripture bridges the alienation from God. Faith, then, is uniquely tied to praxis of that faith in one's life, especially in work that reduces alienation from God and others.

Base communities result in a flattening of hierarchical relationships among group members and the church. The organizational structure reflects an ethic of egalitarianism and cooperation. As Ofelia Schutte describes it: "This [ethical principle] consists of an imperative to treat the other person as one who deserves to be heard regarding the expression of her or his own needs, desires, and ideas" (1993:146). Much more than giving voice to the poor, ideally CEBs should listen as the poor articulate their lives. As opposed to traditional models of church communication, the bottom-up model of CEBs transforms the role of passive believers into active lay participants who interrogate their faith and engage with their social reality. The effects should be revolutionary, an articulation of progressive politics and religious beliefs. It also revises what it means to be a church. Chago, the twenty-eight-year-old youth group sponsor, described the role of the Catholic Church in teaching how to live as a community, especially as expressed in the idea of CEBs:

> CHAGO: I consider that it might be a bit of a Christian education that one comes to have, that one comes to have this kind of vision toward society or community. Because, for example, the Catholic Church always teaches a person to live in the community, to live for the common cause, to always be available so that one can collaborate with and can help others. And I believe that here [in the neighborhood], very little, that is, very little of this exists. So, what I return to and repeat, what I tell you is conscience, many times conscience is lacking. What is the plan God has directly with man? I consider that the plan of God with man is where there exists respect, where there exists brotherhood, where there exists love, understanding, and all of this. And the Catholic Church, I think that it influences us in this way. But, sadly, it's very difficult to make changes in the way people live their lives. I believe it's very difficult.

Despite how difficult it may be to reach the type of communion Chago describes, he believes no attempt would even be made without the presence of the church, especially the presence of groups like CEBs and the youth group, in people's lives. Without the presence of the church, Chago believes, we would not know God's plan of love and fraternity for humankind. Meeting in groups allows for this communion with others, offers a space to reflect on God's message, and models relationships among participants based on an individual's relationship with God. The discourse that circulates in these meetings provides the appropriate metaphors for understanding and describing one's relationship with God.

Talk of God

For members of Belén's Catholic youth group, the model of their relationship with God and their ideals of what it means to relate to others intersect. In their interviews, youths most often described this sentiment using the metaphor of developing a friendship with God. Just as CEB meetings should allow for egalitarian participation and flatten the hierarchical relationships within the church, so too, theologically, group participants should place their relationships with God in more intimate and less authoritative terms. In the following quote, Delfina responds to my question regarding what she enjoys about Catholic youth group. She casts her response in terms of the friendships she has forged with other members of the youth group.

> DELFINA: For example, when I'm sad and I know that I'm going to go to [youth] group, well, I get excited because I'm going to see my friends, my only friends. Come what may, they've always been with me in the good and the bad. So, it makes me happy.

Following this, I asked her to describe what it means to have faith as a Catholic. Her response neatly parallels the way she described youth group:

> DELFINA: Catholic faith is when one has, let's say, faith in that which will always be there and never slip from your hands. That which lets you go and trust in him and tell him your [desires], like a friend, the faith [you'd have with a] friend. I think that faith is something that you've always had, faith that you're going to have [what you ask for]. And it's really very complicated to have faith, because at times one has very little faith, and at times you don't grow because of fear, for fear that the things that you ask for are not going to happen.

For Delfina, friendships within the group and friendship with God both rely on a sense of faith that both God and your friends will come through for you. She relies on the youth group as her closest friends for emotional support when she has problems. God is also a confidant, someone to whom she can entrust her problems and have the confidence that he will not chastise her or abandon her. Delfina believes that her faith in her relationship with God falters only when she fears that he will not come through for her. But if she trusts God as she does her friends, and her friends always come through for her, God too will never fail.

Casting God as a friend was the most common way Catholic youth talked about their relationship with the divine. As a recurring metaphor, God as friend sets up parallel relationships that feed into one another. On one level, friends, or those that make up one's closest community, merit the same respect with which one approaches God. On a celestial level, God deserves the same form of intimacy and confidence with which one approaches one's friends. But God, being the divine, warrants more respect and more intimacy than one's friends. Take, for instance, how Marcos moves from discussing the traits of a good friend to the fact that God is the only true friend he possesses, in the sense of having someone with whom to share his most grave troubles:

MARCOS: Look, for me, I think it would be sincerity, then, or trust, because let's say sometimes you have a true friend, right, and he or she comes and tells you sentimentally what happened, and with the trust that you aren't going to tell [anyone else]. Let's say I have a friend like this. I tell him, right, "Look, I have this problem," or "Look, there's this girl here." But, you already know [about her]. You don't say anything to me. "Right, man, no we're not going to say anything," he tells me. And here he comes and tells me about his stuff, too. And so we keep it between us. And I believe that this is the best [kind of friendship], then, to have sincerity and trust. For me, this is friendship, the best kind of friendship that one can have with a friend.

JON: When you have a problem who do you turn to for advice?

MARCOS: When I have problems like this, just me, Jon. I never let anyone know when I have a problem. I manage. I guard my problems. I look for the way and to God, right, to overcome them.

JON: You ask God to counsel you?

MARCOS: Yes, one talks to him always for everything, and so in this way we overcome the problem. But, depending on the problems, I don't confess them to a friend in that way. If the problems are such that they aren't very important, yes, one tells one's friends. But the really serious problems, in such a way, no, no. I don't like to tell problems such as these [to others].

It may seem trite that Marcos views God as his only true confidant for serious personal problems, yet the serial manner in which Marcos (and other youth) connects his relationship with his friends to his relationship with God demonstrates how salient this fact is for him. Ideally, confidence between friends should be such that one knows the other person will not gossip to others about what was said. The circle, as Marcos describes such a friendship, should be closed. Yet Marcos says he does not have such relationships in his life; he feels he can trust no one in this way, except God. Marcos insinuates that this is so because God will not blab to others about your problems. And it is not that you trust friends like you would God, but rather that you trust God like you would your best of friends. A direct and personal relationship with God is modeled on a relationship between intimate equals. Unlike in many versions of evangelicalism in Latin America, Catholic youth and CEBs do not cast God as a paternal, distant, and castigating figure, nor as an emperor or powerful political figure. Of all the relationship imagery available to draw upon, a Catholic CEB's emphasis on equality of social position transfers to the way in which members like Marcos envision the style and type of relationship they have with the divine—one of mutual respect, cooperation, and friendship. It is a relationship of mutual love.

To Love God

The theme of loving God is an important recurring trope used in the New Testament. Jesus' ministry is one based on mutual love between people and emphasizes the love God has for humankind. This New Testament focus on love was a frequent topic of discussion during youth group meetings and church services, and even spontaneously found its way into conversations about faith. For example, during one youth group meeting, Roberto and Delfina led a discussion on the "God Is Love" selection from the Bible, introducing their topic under the title: "God-Love Is the Fountain of Love (*Dios Amor es la fuente de amor*)." Roberto read the passage from 1 John 4:7–12 (NIV):

> Dear friends, let us love one another, for love comes from God. Everyone who loves has been born of God and knows God. Whoever does not love does not know God, because God is love. This is how God showed his love among us: He sent his one and only Son into the world that we might live through him. This is love: not that we loved God, but that he loved us and sent his Son as an atoning sacrifice for our sins. Dear friends, since God so loved us, we also ought to love one another. No one has ever seen God; but if we love one another, God lives in us and his love is made complete in us.

Through either direct or indirect quoting, many of my Catholic friends invoked the ideas in this passage to convey the double relationship between God and humans that love demands. I say double relationship because the directive to love demands love of God and love of others simultaneously. Indeed, one cannot be present without the other.

When Roberto called upon other group members to discuss what the passage meant to them, many simply reasserted the obvious points of the passage, saying, "God is love," or "To know God is to know love." Victoria, however, took her analysis deeper into what it means to love one another. She tied the passage to more immediate concerns by responding, "I think too that if there was more trust (*confianza*) between ourselves and if we loved each other more, there wouldn't be so much delinquency today."

Her choice of words is instructive. The term *confianza* in Spanish is most often translated as "trust," but it has a secondary meaning of "camaraderie," a meaning that resonates strongly with ideals of friendship. In essence, Victoria relates the current social climate of crime to a lack of friendliness and trust in society, both being at the root of love. Her comment alludes to the unspoken connection between love for others and love for God. She believes that in order to demonstrate our love for God, we must also interact, as a society or community, with love. Victoria believes this is precisely what the majority of Hondurans are not doing, and that their lack of trust and charity foments crime.

Chago, replying to Victoria, offers Jesus as the model for learning about love: "Practically do what Jesus did—this is how we understand love—by respecting others, giving to others. In this group we have to always renew this love between us." If Chago's suggestion to act as Jesus seems a bit unattainable, a bit too lofty for humans, he tempers this by saying that the youth group is the community in which mimicking the acts of Jesus and living out Jesus' words can take place. It emphasizes the human aspects of Jesus, as opposed to the divine, in such a way that the historical personage of Jesus and his acts give us a path to follow as moral signposts that should direct our behavior. By using Jesus as a human model, Chago points to the ethical prescriptions that one must adhere to in order to live a life dedicated to the service of one's community and sharing in daily struggles. In other words, an ethic of love for others is one that follows Jesus' example.

Moral Signposts and Acts of Love

Victoria, in using the term *confianza* to characterize the ideal type of relationship members of society should have with one another, and Marcos, who places his relationship with God in terms of camaraderie, both exemplify the type of love for others characterized by Jesus in the New Testament. Just as Jesus practiced acts of love within a religious community—his disciples and followers—Christian love must be practiced, not just believed. Repeatedly, Catholic youths' connection to the neighborhood from the point of view of the youth group rested precisely on the acts of love they performed. Again, taking their relationship with God based on a model of friendliness as their cue, Catholic youths articulated that without demonstrating love to others you could not demonstrate love for God. Youths manifested love toward others in the service they carried out in their community. Such an idea is based on an understanding of a theology of accompaniment as solidarity *with* the community in which you live.

Chago made this connection between the life of Jesus and the work of the group in a discussion we had about how Belén's youth group distinguished itself from others:

CHAGO: I've always thought that you can't be beating yourself up all the time inside the church when others suffer in the street; you can't be speaking about loving your neighbor when we don't practice it outside of church; where we're talking of forgiveness when we don't forgive others outside of church; where we're speaking about love when we don't love outside of church. And I say that Jesus preached. He preached, but he loved, but he forgave, but he acted, but he healed. So, if he, being God, did these things, why don't we? If this is our obligation, it is our obligation as Christians to do it. So, I say that the group, the group distinguishes itself as different from other groups that I know in this way.

In his statement, Chago draws together the acts of Jesus with the standards of involvement in the community that the youth group holds for itself. He describes an active involvement with the community, an engagement with community life that also engages questions of faith. Chago believes that it is not enough to hold onto belief or to talk about love and forgiveness, but that we must also perform acts of love in our everyday lives. To do otherwise is hypocritical. It is an elaboration of a common refrain I heard from my Catholic friends: a work of charity without faith is fruitless (and conversely, faith without works of charity is also fruitless).

In his statement, Chago also tears down the barrier between the church and the community. He wants to actively take the church beyond its walls and its meetings and insert it into the neighborhood streets. For the Catholic youth group this meant that living their faith involved working in solidarity with their community. As a group, they would carry out a number of social projects. These included cleaning up the trash from the ravine, cleaning the church building, fund-raising for the sick and poor, visiting friends and church members who had fallen ill or were dying, and, above all, being a presence in the community. As a group, they would attend funerals and vigils and petition prayers for the health and well-being of those in the neighborhood. Teresa described this relationship by using the New Testament parable of the mustard seed, drawing parallels between the group's works in the neighborhood and one's faith:

> TERESA: Faith, faith is, well for me it's very important, right, because I believe that we have to, all of us, we have to have faith. And like they say, if we had faith like a little mustard seed if we were sick, we would get better and everything. We could accomplish many things. The truth is that faith is very important. But at times, I think that not all of us, not all of us have faith. Or that we have very little faith because it is not only having faith, but faith, like it says in the Bible, faith has to be accompanied by actions, not only faith, that I have faith that God exists. All this is important, but you also have to help out, to see how you can help the community. Or when we go out, if you meet someone then, to see how, in what way we can serve them. It's not just believing that God exists, but the two must go hand and hand.

Both Teresa and Chago develop the idea that working in the community is a sign of one's faith in God. In fact, community works are the manifestation of a strong faith, a moral signpost to others that one has strong faith in God and faith in the community. Faith in and of itself requires a demonstration of love. And what better way to demonstrate this quality of love to both God and the community than through one's ethical actions? Teresa alludes to the New Testament parable of the mustard seed (Luke 13:18–19) to describe this faith. Something so small as a mustard seed, the parable explains, can grow into a tall and vibrant plant. Any work within the community done out of faith, no matter how small and insignificant it may seem at its inception, can flower into something large and healthy. If work is done out of faith, it can have unlimited potential.

Having such unshakable faith, however, is not always easy. Members of the Catholic youth group recognized that although they would like to live their faith through their works in the community, there are many social and personal impediments to doing so. Aware that living a theology of accompaniment means sharing in common struggles with others in their community, Catholic youth also know that sharing the struggles of other youth, especially gang youth, is a dangerous enterprise. Although they have incorporated the church's concern for living in and as a part of the community, church youth meet the challenge of doing so ambivalently in the face of youth violence. For church youth, solidarity with and identification as poor or working class is the easier thing to do. This stems from CEBs' historical concern for economic injustice. However, in the neoliberal climate of Honduras, many other social problems accompany economic injustice. The root cause of youth violence and gang involvement, according to these Catholics, is the dismal economic future faced by young men and women.

The Neoliberal Challenge to CEBs

The social science literature most often describes CEBs as offering a sense of solidarity to the poor as they confront economic injustices. CEBs readily organize to address issues of economic disparity and exploitation, critiquing elites for their abuse of power. One of the more critical features of CEB concerns is the emphasis that God does not condone unequal distribution of wealth and political and economic exploitation. This is a crucial shift in other forms of Catholic belief (both traditional and folk) in which poverty is a punishment for one's wicked ways or lack of faith. Poverty, this view suggests, is something one accepts as one's lot in life.

The progressive church, in organizing CEBs, actively seeks to overturn this image with an emphasis on Jesus' commitment to the poor and his social critique of excessive wealth, especially at the expense of others. In this view, the poor are poor because of social oppression. Only through solidarity, or identification with the poor, does the critique of economic inequality gather its force. Part of the critique is a moral judgment against those who hold wealth and maintain their position through the exploitation of others.

In the neoliberal climate of Latin America, we would imagine that CEBs would gather greater strength because of their social critique of economic disparity. However, this has not proven to be the case. Instead, perhaps because of the greater demands on meeting daily survival caused by neoliberal policies, CEB participation has lagged region-wide. I propose, however, that this is only a partial explanation. In addition, neoliberal ideologies of individual comparative advantage have eroded a sense of community and working together. That is, an emphasis on individualism has atomized cooperation and civic participation. Neoliberalism is an economic plan that has succeeded in exacerbating a bevy of social problems, including youth violence. CEBs' basic critique of economic injustice and repression attempts to address the ancillary problems associated with neoliberal reforms. In the following excerpt from a youth group meeting, we can see the tensions between neoliberal ideologies of individualism and an understanding that problems such as youth violence stem from economic conditions.

Fieldnotes, May 20, 2002. Saturday evening I went to Catholic youth group. We met in the parish building, as usual, the light blue walls illuminated by the bare fluorescent bulbs. Through the bars on the windows, we could hear the neighborhood watching their soap operas and listening to their music. The evening's theme for discussion was violence and insecurity in Honduras. Marcos led the meeting. The first question he asked was, What factors favor the increase in violence and delinquency in the country?

Chago said that violence and delinquency in the country is due to a number of factors: family disintegration, poverty, the mistreatment of children by their parents, and then there is corruption in the sense of organized crime, of which "the military, the government—all of them are messed up in it." Others in the group echoed Chago, emphasizing that the main causes of delinquency and violence are poverty and the lack of work. As if to provide a biblical context in which to understand why the world is as it is, Chago explained that "the word of Christ says that he doesn't come to bring peace, but to bring war, a battle against corruption and oppression of the poor." In other words, we should read some of the current violence, especially violence to end economic injustice, as Christ's presence in the world, struggling on behalf of the poor.

Marcos continued, asking, "How do you think the government can overcome the problem of delinquency?" This question created a rift in the group.

Eber was the first to speak out. I have to keep in mind that Eber and his family are not the typical residents of Belén. His family is much wealthier than most. Eber attends a private university in San Pedro Sula, studying computer technology and business. He doesn't have to work.

His political views are also, generally, a lot more conservative than those of other group members, especially on economic issues. I don't know if he was being serious when he gave his reply, but it is certainly representative of a thread of sentiment in this country. How should the government counter the rise in delinquency? Eber replied succinctly: "Simple. Kill all the gang members. Put all the members of the gang 18 and the gang 13 in the same room and let them kill each other."

At first, no one directly commented on or refuted Eber's strong statement. I was taken aback, as I never expected to hear such an unsympathetic and uncompassionate view from a member of the group. Marcos, as if ignoring Eber's reply, said that the key to ending delinquency is to give people work—people turn to crime in the first place because there are no jobs.[2] Many of the group members groaned at this, and a chorus of voices bemoaned, "But there is no work in this country!"

Eber, however, insisted that there is work. He is the only one; all the others were saying that work is very hard to come by—good work, that is, which pays a decent wage.

Again, no one directly challenged Eber's view. Instead, Elizabeth gave the example of a parish-sponsored NGO and how it was trying to rehabilitate gang members by teaching them skills and job training. But Eber's voice overpowered Elizabeth's, drowning her out by repeatedly asking in a louder and louder voice, "How can a *marero* change, tell me? Can he change? Tell me how?" His unwillingness to believe in rehabilitation connects with his solution of killing off all the gang members in the country to end crime.

The argument shifted back to whether or not there is work in Honduras. Eber kept insisting there is, saying that the maquilas, for instance, pay very good money and that workers are lazy, that's why there is such a high turnover. Carolina, who had been sitting quietly, spoke out in a trembling voice, as if she were trying to keep her self-control, "Only some of the maquilas pay well, Eber. And it is hard work."

Eber interrupted her, asking rhetorically, "Well, you expect not to work hard?"

"Many times the workers are mistreated," Carolina finished. She should know; she works at a maquila outside of town.

But Eber stubbornly refused to concede anything. Finally, as if she didn't want to have to resort to bringing it up, Carolina almost spit out, "You think it's so easy? You should try working in a maquila for a day and see how easy it is."

A direct hit to Eber's position of privilege. He stormed out of the parish building.

Afterwards, I heard from many who were there that Eber needs to hear these things, that he needs to understand, because he is going to be in management and could forget his friends' economic situation.

We can take Eber's strong statements as to the solution to youth violence and the employment situation in Honduras as emblematic of certain political threads in the country. Whereas other group members tie together youth violence and youth unemployment as crucial in understanding juvenile delinquency and crime, Eber's explanation draws from two interrelated beliefs. First, gang youth are irredeemable and cannot be rehabilitated. This is a sentiment that sometimes serves to justify state and para-state murders of gang youth as well as a continued disinvestment from the types of social programming that could offer youth an alternative to gang life. Second, Eber's insistence that job opportunities in Honduras for young men and women exist (even as most of his friends in the youth group struggled to find gainful and long-term employment) delegitimizes the group's understanding that violence is a symptom of economic oppression. Indeed, in his statements, Eber rejects that God is on the side of the oppressed, a fundamental underpinning of a theology of accompaniment. Instead, Eber criticizes the work ethic of youth, citing that the maquila industry, as the best employment opportunity for young men and women, has a high rate of turnover because of young people's laziness and unwillingness to work hard, not because of the oppressive work conditions noted by Carolina.

Eber ultimately reinforces neoliberal ideologies about individualism in both of his explanations. Gangs exist because of individual, delinquent youth who are unaffected by political and economic realities that might influence them to enter gang life. Unemployment is a problem only because individual youth do not look hard enough for the myriad of job opportunities supposedly available. The reason that youth never make headway in their economic and personal lives is that they are lazy and expect their futures to come easy to them. Eber leaves little room for a political economic critique of youth violence.

Other members of the youth group, however, reject the atomizing logic of neoliberalism, in favor of an explanation that demonstrates their solidarity with other working-class and working-poor youth. Due to his economic position, Eber becomes a stand-in for the wealthy and provides one of the only opportunities for the other youth to talk back directly to the powerful. They know that Eber is not one of the elites, at least not yet, but they hope to impress upon him what they perceive to be the largest problem for their generation, a lack of opportunities. Perhaps in the future, when Eber is in the corporate world, he will remember what they tried to tell him and treat his workers with dignity.

In their replies to Eber, group members specifically highlight the position of structural exclusion that youths in Honduras share, regardless of whether they are gang members or churchgoers. However, what they fail to articulate is why they, who also face similar problems of unemployment and underemployment, do not lead lives of crime. At some level, the answer is self-evident: they aren't gang members because they are members of the Catholic youth group instead. Because they have found social support through church activities, these struggling, working-class youth don't need the gang. However, they are acutely aware that, like gang members, they are affected by structural inequalities. Social support from the church helps alleviate attenuation. Together, they can work as a community for greater change, at least within their neighborhood, but working together at the community level can have only limited impact on national and global politics.

The sentiments expressed at this meeting were the closest identification with gang youth I heard from my Catholic friends. By providing economic reasons for the problem of gangs, they also included themselves, perhaps inadvertently, as those affected by such injustices. In this meeting, we witness the ambiguity of these Catholic youths' positions. At times, they wish to identify themselves with all youth but also want to maintain a critical distance between themselves and gang members. No one in the group would defend the violence of gang members. But neither would they exclude gang members from sharing similar problems with all youth. Group members' own understanding of accompaniment is at odds with the world of gang violence. In essence, two moral communities collide, and it is up to Catholic youth to reconcile their religious belief with their actions in the community.

Moral Communities and Acts of Violence

According to the Argentine sociologist Carlos Torres (1992), within a society there will be contestations over what constitutes ethical practice. Although Torres views ethical fissures as occurring most often along lines

of economic class, as in Eber's understanding of the causes of youth violence explored above, this need not always be the case. Ethical differences
occur within the same community, along lines of age and gender. For
Torres, organized religion attempts to homogenize these disparate ethical beliefs through the standardization of definitions of ethical behavior.
Religion acts as a leveling institution, flattening the ethical differences
between social classes and establishing itself as a moral authority.

In this sense, religious belief organizes communities of believers
through the ethical prescriptions they follow. Where a plurality of religions exists, believers use ethical differences to distinguish themselves
from others. Even in cases in which the ethics and morals performed are
fundamentally the same or use the same source for belief, like the Bible,
the critical differences are what set groups apart as moral communities.
In the case of contemporary forms of Catholicism as practiced in many
places in Latin America, an ethic of companionship (or accompaniment) has altered what it means to be a community of believers and
how to enact that community, and brought about new ways of modeling one's relationship with God. It is an ethic of community solidarity. As explored through the above quotations from Belén's Catholic
youth group, solidarity signifies working and living one's faith through
outreach to others, struggling alongside members of one's community
regardless of social status, and performing acts of love in line with Jesus'
teachings. Community solidarity is a major component of one's Catholic faith.

But when faced with youth violence in the community, acts of solidarity and identification with the oppressed become dangerous iden-
tifications for youth to make. Solidarity and accompaniment normally
entail a shared journey and identification as a common community.
However, if Catholic youth identify with all youth—including addicted
and violent youth—this places them in a situation of possibly being
confused *with* this class of youth. The ethical ideal may be solidarity,
but an uneasy tension exists between wanting to demonstrate com-
passionate understanding for others and wanting to maintain enough
difference to avoid confusion. Youth group members must reconcile
their belief in solidarity with how they feel they can act safely in the
neighborhood. It is a reconciliation that relies on the concept of faith
in action.

Delfina expresses this tension in the comment below. Notice how
she vacillates between what she sees as her youth group's duty to be a

resource for those young men and women who want to change their violent lives and her fears regarding the possible consequences of doing so.

DELFINA: That's why gang members exist. Because at times we're not so brave to go where they are and say to them that we invite them [to the youth group] because of a fear of approaching them they might go and do something to us or say something. But I believe that we have to have friendship with them, as well, because they are human beings. And that they are, some of them are repentant, but they don't leave [the gang] because no one's there to support them. That's why, because they think that they're nobodies . . . I imagine that God is always there for them when they repent. He never leaves anyone alone.

It is not that Delfina believes gang members cannot change their violent behavior, but rather that they rarely find support from the community to do so. She recognizes that it is her own and other community members' fear that may prevent gang youth from finding the support they need. She believes that gang members deserve the same type of friendship as should be given to others in the community. Notice how she recognizes that her failure to offer the kind of friendship she shares with others is compensated for by the support God offers. Even though she may fail gang members, God will always be there if they choose to accept him.

In his interview, Fernando comments that relating to gang youth takes a special kind of evangelizing and hence requires a special kind of relationship that is different from the kind he has with other youth. He partially breaks with an ideal of accompaniment by wanting to give gang youth different treatment. Implicit in his statement is that he and his friends may not be prepared, in terms of their faith, to evangelize to gangs.

FERNANDO: Well, the hope always exists that a person who has fallen [from grace] might change, right? But, but many times someone who's fallen doesn't get back on track. And it depends on the kind of gospel that is given to them, because one must know how to evangelize, too, right? But, I say, many times when one has fallen, he doesn't have [the means] to return to a normal life. Because, let's say, a gang member, a gang member that hasn't killed—because the thought of a gang member is to kill those from other gangs—and I say that, that he doesn't know how to reason. He isn't rational like other people [are]. That is, he only thinks about killing those from other gangs, because that's what I've heard about gang members. That they only think about killing and stealing and doing nothing, because gang members don't do anything. They don't work; they steal. So, I don't know, I don't know how we can get someone back to a normal way of life once they've lost their way. I don't know.

Fernando finds it impossible to conceive of the idea that a gang member is not a murderer or a thief. His knowledge about gangs relies on the stories others have told concerning gang behavior. Through these stories, Fernando concludes that such people have lost the capacity for moral reasoning because they exist beyond the influence of God and society. Gangs and churches are distinct moral communities, despite their members sharing a common identity based on age and class. Fernando is at a loss as to what the appropriate course of action would be to bring gang members back to a normal life. He knows that God can help them, but he does not know if he could be a conduit to help bring about that change. He cannot bridge the moral differences between his community and that of gang members.

Meanwhile, Eber's outburst may have had something to do with this inability to see the point of view of gang members. Instead of exploring the possibility of rehabilitation, which would also require him to dwell on his own deficiencies, Eber rejects the idea of solidarity altogether.

Youth group members want to serve their community through a belief in accompaniment, and yet they know the limits of being able to do so. Despite assurances at the CEB meeting, Arturo readily articulated this sentiment. Being a gang member, he knew how difficult it would be for others to see beyond his past acts and to incorporate him more fully into the community. This is a concern that comes out in Eber's callous comments at the youth group meeting described above. For these reasons, Arturo's comments that someone should change only out of his own desire resonates more deeply with the limits of Catholic sentiments and their claims to being the predominant moral community. Arturo feels that society—even Catholics in his own community—rejects them while simultaneously desiring that something be done about gangs. Arturo also uses the community's indifferent approach toward him and other gang members. Indeed, through his acts and way of behaving in the neighborhood, Arturo cultivates a reserved, distant relationship with others. Gang members use the reticence of the community as an excuse for behaving the way they do. These entrenched, complementary views create a wider breach between the two.

This does not go unnoticed, however, by more astute members of the Catholic community. Chago recognizes that the community's reaction and behavior toward gang members is what alienates gang youth from living as part of the moral community envisioned and practiced by Catholics. In this sense, this community of Catholics fails to live its faith fully as God would want. Its inability to demonstrate love toward gang members reflects their inability to fully love God.

> CHAGO: For days now, I come home and see a young man who's in a gang. And I've come home, like, two or three times and I always see him eating outside. His aunt gives him a plate of food when he goes to ask for it, but he is always outside. He's always on a corner, not inside the house. And I say that if their own family rejects them, then without a doubt other people are going to reject them [gang members] too. And I say that the relationship is very bad. It is definitely bad. In a certain way, I think that it's understandable, because here people don't care for gang members. Also because, well, for example, here they've killed people, people much loved in the community. I always tell people, it's not about hating them, it's not about hating them, it's about understanding them and to see in what way. . . . And, I say that it's in accordance with how I've lived. It's what I say to people, that seeing them with hate isn't the way [to live].

The simple act of gang members' families refusing them a place to eat is metaphoric of the relationship that gang members have with the community as a whole: you can have your meal, but you must sit outside. For Chago this is a powerful statement about the level of rancor and hate that others have for gang members, because it isolates them even more and precludes understanding and communication. It is justifiable, perhaps, but it drives a wedge between the community and some of its youth. The statement is made more poignant by the fact that Chago was alluding to Arturo as the young man who is forced to eat outside. Chago has seen how families reject their gang member sons and grandsons, and hence the whole of the community rejects them as well. In Chago's view, the way to counter gang growth is to foster a sense of belonging to the community and build cooperation among youths and the neighborhood. Chago's concern over the gang members being left on the outside of community life explains Arturo's presence at the CEB meeting described earlier. Chago invited Arturo to the meeting in hope of demonstrating to him that despite how he behaves, Arturo is still welcome to the support offered by the community. Arturo, in his stubbornness, or in his understanding of community sentiment, chose not to listen.

Toward a Theology of Forgiveness

In the face of such grave social problems as youth violence, the Catholic Church's theology of accompaniment with the poor and dispossessed—in other words, its identification with the communities in which the church finds itself located—proves to have contradictory outcomes. At once, it provides for a communal feeling, creating solidarity with all who share their same position in life, while failing to make distinctions within that community, because such distinctions are considered immoral. There is a profound sense of equality before God. So all poor are united because they are poor, all women are united because they are women, and all young people—gang members or not—are united because they are young people. The solidarity cannot offer sanctuary from violence, because of the implied homogeneity of the grouping. However, the call for community solidarity, precisely because it provides a space for everyone—including the violent, gangs, and people with addictions—cannot offer protective shelter for those who need physical and emotional respite from violence. Being one with the community, they cannot break away from identification with vice and violent behaviors. Catholics, by viewing themselves as "the community" under which all segments of the population fall, have little recourse to alter an individual's behavior in the way that evangelical Protestantism offers its adherents a conceptual separation from the sins of the world (see chapter 5). Indeed, because CEB participants are likely to contend that sin is social—including violence and drug addiction—they offer only incorporation into the community, not a radical break from the community.

Belén's Catholic youth group may not be able to provide succor for violent youth. However, this community does provide a social prophylactic of sorts by offering space for youth to develop critical awareness of the problems around them. CEB and youth group participation offer young men and women space in their community at a time when public space for youth is diminishing (see chapter 2). Inserting youth into the community through church participation keeps them in the public eye at a time when they are actively and violently erased from public view by youth violence. Catholic youths provide a visible, countervailing image of Honduran working-class youth, one not immediately associated with violence.

CEB and youth group participation encourages them to both reflect on their problems and act on them. By emphasizing a faith based on community works, youth insert themselves into their community and provide a countervailing image of youth, reminding others of their heterogeneity even as they assert a certain commonality of position. But perhaps the most radical benefit of all is teaching youths that living *with* the community is a crucial component of living in communion with God. Youths strive to approach community relations with the same sense of love and friendship they know they feel toward God. Embedded in their relationship with God is the idea that just as God forgives our sins, so we, too, must forgive the sins of others, even if we critique what they do as wrong. This is an aspect of one's relationship to God and community that youths address with a popular theology of forgiveness. Although forgiveness of others is not the same as acceptance, true forgiveness is a seed, like Teresa's mustard seed, that can grow strong to provide the beginnings of reconciliation. Forgiveness, when done from the heart and without hypocrisy, entails the radical love of God and others, as well as an end to animosity. Forgiveness fails when we fail to forgive completely. Or, as Martín voiced this sentiment:

> MARTÍN: For example, some people say that only God forgives. "I don't have to forgive you because only God forgives." So, these people are living wrong. They're not living according to the Word. So, I feel that they don't have peace, because if they say this, if someone then offended them, then, there cannot be a change in them, because they might be holding a grudge. They can't change this rancor because, as they say, only God, then only God has to entrust himself with this, and they don't. And it is completely opposite, because the Word, when it speaks of forgiveness, for example the Word, the Our Father prayer says "forgive us our trespasses as we forgive those who trespass against us." Or when Peter asked Jesus, "How many times do I have to forgive my brother?" Seven times, Peter said. And Jesus told him no, seven times no, seventy times seven times. This means you must always forgive your brother.

During that inaugural CEB meeting I attended, this dynamic of forgiveness and acceptance was evident. José Luis, in search for forgiveness of his past as a gang member, realized that he first had to forgive himself. The sins that stained him were his past actions, sins that he committed against the community, but which he had to first reconcile with himself.

Then he could turn to the community for absolution. Arturo, however, recognized that forgiveness by others is always partial. He knew that the accumulation of his past deeds would not be easily erased. At the youth group meeting described above, Eber's unwillingness to believe that gang members are able to reform also stems from the inability to forgive them of their past deeds. Despite the fact that other youth, such as Martín, feel they must always forgive one another, extending forgiveness to those who have killed their family members and friends or for whom friends and family have been murdered because of mistaken identity, remains difficult. Perhaps because of the internal changes within communities in Latin America, progressive Catholic teachings have begun to reemphasize forgiveness along with solidarity. Mitigating the pain of social violence in communities will entail a radical theology of forgiveness so that both perpetrators and victims of violence may move forward. Otherwise, solidarity may paradoxically foster the acceptance and inevitability of violence.

Conclusion

Burdick's (1993) ethnography of religious participation in a community outside of Rio de Janeiro reevaluates the role of CEBs in relation to progressive political ideals. Focusing on class and political participation, Burdick argues that CEBs are not successful in addressing issues of gender (such as domestic violence) and racism. Overall, CEBs as practiced do not represent a true break from society, despite the ideology of liberation behind CEB organizing. Burdick's findings are not directly applicable to the situation I have described. It is not that CEBs do not address issues other than economic exploitation. Indeed, women's and youth groups based on the CEB model readily attempt to address other forms of exploitation. Rather, CEBs are less effective in addressing other forms of exploitation because of the ambiguity that arises when applying such a critique within their own community. CEB members who adhere to a belief in the theology of accompaniment must reconcile critiques of their own community members, with whom they should be in solidarity, and the desire to have others conform to their ethical standards. In other words, to offer a valid critique we must view ourselves as separate from that which we are critiquing, yet how can we do that if we are to be in solidarity with those who are being critiqued?

Although class differences between the rich and the poor are common topics for Catholic meetings modeled on CEBs, the inability of

CEBs to address issues of violence more fully stems from their inclusive theology of accompaniment. Economic violence, even in a neoliberal climate, is more readily critiqued because the moral distinctions being made are less ambiguous. You can critique the exploitation of labor, an international system that maintains unequal distribution of wealth, and elites who hoard resources, because it is clear that they are not living up to their moral obligations toward God and society. "They" are spatially distant from those who make the critique. On a more intimate scale, it becomes difficult to make such distinctions without violating, in some way, an ethic of inclusion. For youth group members, love and compassion become more difficult to apply when wrongs are committed against them by their neighbors. Group members, in essence, ask, "How is it possible to remain critical of others' ethical failings if we simultaneously love and accept them as part of our own moral community?" For them, forgiveness and acceptance by others are only partially offered. They realize that total forgiveness of others' wrongs is a near impossibility for them: only God offers complete and unconditional absolution. Acceptance is also only partial because of the ambiguity and danger involved in a complete acceptance of those who have violated social norms, as demonstrated in the ambiguous response of Catholic youth in evangelizing to gang youth and incorporating them into their social networks.

It is telling that José Luis ultimately turned to Pentecostalism in search of the forgiveness and acceptance he sought. Because of Pentecostalism's decidedly separate orientation from the rest of the community in terms of doctrine and practice, it is able to offer sanctuary for those young men who wish to leave gang life. Incorporation into the Pentecostal church structure is total and asks for immediate reform of all vice. Sin, because it is personal and not social, must be reconciled only between the individual and God, not among community members. Although youths must constantly demonstrate to others their personal reformation through their bodily and social habits, and although suspicion of former gang youths takes time to diminish, they rely less on others in affirming their absolved status. I turn to this dilemma in the next chapter.

5
Finding Sanctuary
Youth Violence and Pentecostalism

The Mark of a Dedicated Christian

It was unbearably muggy that Sunday, even for a June evening. I was thankful that the God Is Love Pentecostal Church had moved from its tiny storefront, badly ventilated and with broken fans, to the new, more spacious building. "Building" might be an exaggeration. The steel beams and supports had been raised and the corrugated tin roof placed, but the church still lacked the ubiquitous cinder-block walls. The church was being built entirely of volunteer labor, mostly young men, and although they raised the roof in less than three months, there were indications that progress would slow. Many of the young men felt they should be paid something for their work, that they had given enough already, and if the church wanted construction to continue, they would have to hire someone.

Rows of white plastic lawn chairs sat on the dirt floor. The floor, to spatially mark the inside of the church, was spread with reddish-brown wood chips. A number of young men milled around at the back. They knew that there were never enough seats for everyone. They enthusiastically would participate with loud hoots, blasts on plastic trumpets, and an occasional "*¡Dios es podoroso!*" (God is powerful) and "*Gloria a Dios!*" (Glory to God) (fig. 7). Sitting in the rows facing the front of the church were families, young mothers, older women and men, and groups of young women dressed in their best outfits and high-heeled shoes.

The pastor did not take the stage until the service was almost over. The sermon is nearly the last part of the program, the climax of the evening. The wood pulpit had been moved from the old church building to the new site and set on the makeshift stage. Originally from Tela on the coast, the pastor, in his late thirties, has a powerful voice and a slight limp in his step from childhood polio. He commands attention from his audience. It is not just that he speaks into a microphone hooked up to two oversized, cranked-up speakers that blast his voice across the neighborhood and

Figure 7. Calling members to a Pentecostal evening church service. Photograph by author.

into the night, calling out to the congregation and beyond. His words—his intonation, the modulation in volume—are like violent waves crashing against a rocky shore. He is a force to be reckoned with as he moves from low pitch to shouts that roll in his throat, raspy. I have rarely heard him use a "normal" speaking voice, even in one-on-one conversations. His is a voice that directs, that calls, and that is not afraid to denounce. He began his sermon, introduced as "The Mark of a Consecrated (*consagrado*) Christian," with his characteristic verve:

"*Consagrado* means a person who loves the Lord, to be with him, to be called by him exclusively. The Lord calls the person to be exclusively with him. . . . Also, *consagrado* means someone who is purified, who is in the presence of the Lord, someone who is holy, who has been sanctified. . . . We can't consecrate ourselves, it must be through God, through being purified by him."

He let his voice trail off, pausing dramatically, and then called out, "This is the resource that families need, that a marriage needs, that all is brought to the house of the Lord. . . . God doesn't want your *joven* or *jovencito* [young man] to find himself in the street with a chimba on his chest or an AK [47] on the collarbone. You might be big in society, but this grandeur means nothing before the grandeur of God." The pastor worked his voice into a low shriek, screaming into the microphone, "No one will resist! No one will resist because God sent his only Son to save us!"

The reverberation of the speakers quieted before he began again. "Years ago, at the time of the election of the Reina government, it was said that Honduras was going to change. But I want to say that no one can change his or her life without God! If you find yourself in the street, in the disco, with a chimba in your hands, return to God so that you may adore the Lord." He lifted his Bible to the crowd and quoted Leviticus 10:7 from memory while the congregation eagerly flipped through their own Bibles to find the passage: "'Do not leave the entrance to the Tent of Meeting, or you will die,'" the pastor quoted, "'because the LORD's anointing oil is on you.' So they did as Moses said."

The pastor paced around the platform, hands in the air, exhorting the congregation to take heed, saying, "Do you know when you lose your teenagers? When they leave the house, because the street is poison! Your priority as a young adult is to be in the presence of the Lord. Your priority as a wife is to be in the presence of the Lord. Your priority as a husband is to be in the presence of the Lord. Your priority as a child is to be in the presence of the Lord. Because God doesn't want you to follow the wrong path. Enough already without God! Enough already without Christ!

"The psychology of the person who is not consecrated is outside of the house of God. . . . Parents, if you don't want your children to find themselves in gangs, in drugs, in prostitution, be an example and come to Christ. . . . The soul of that delinquent, that kidnapper, that rapist, is the soul of God too. Christ wants you! Christ wants you! If you mothers [can] no longer bear your sons being in drugs, in delinquency, search for life in Jesus."

The transformative power of the Pentecostal Church, especially in confronting social violence, is deftly expressed in the above sermon excerpt delivered by the head pastor of a church in Colonia Belén. In the sermon, the pastor weaves together the theme of Christian dedication through church involvement with the reality of everyday social violence as it particularly affects youth. Here, drawing on some key metaphors within the Pentecostal faith, the pastor invokes the necessary role of God and Pentecostalism in transforming the social practices of youth. He adroitly includes youth (among others) in his version of social change while he atomizes participation, individualizing the response to youth violence as a personal one, not collective or community oriented. Yet within this individualized approach resides a paradox: it is only through living as a "dedicated Christian" that one demonstrates to others the power of individual (personal) change in transforming society. Conversion of oneself and others falls short if practice (dedication) is lacking.

In the previous chapter, I explored how the Catholic Church's orientation toward community life offers models of community participation for young men and women. Youth, through participation in Catholic youth group and CEBs, grow closer to their community and understand their faith as living through their actions there. I have argued that Catholic youth seek social change through their acts in the world and thus cannot regard themselves as spatially or conceptually distinct from others in the community. In this chapter, I examine the dialogue between Pentecostal churches and community youth in developing responses to youth violence. Conversion to evangelical faiths for some youth is a way of overcoming "poisonous" social environments, such as the street, and the forms of violence that youth encounter there. While conversion is about saving the soul from eternal damnation, it is also about receiving God's blessing in this world through being physically saved from danger. I argue that conversion is a process, an ongoing demonstration of one's "state of grace." Young men use the spatial metaphors provided by the Pentecostal Church, which organize the social and spiritual worlds into broad categories of safety and danger, and deploy them in a way that provides succor from youth violence. Conversion is a particular strategy for some young men that lifts them out of the violence of the everyday and reinscribes them into a new and protective social space (Lefebvre 1991) in the church. Pentecostal youth draw on these metaphors in constructing a safe space that informs their interaction with other youth. The safety afforded by association with evangelical churches is contingent upon the degree of "seriousness" that young Pentecostals demonstrate in their beliefs and actions to the broader community.

Latin American Evangelicalism and the Promise of Salvation

To understand the position of the evangelical Protestant faiths in Honduras as they relate to young men and women in particular, we must first understand the broad characteristics of the promise of salvation offered by these faiths. Although evangelical Protestant faiths are concerned with the state of the eternal soul, believing that only through offering oneself to Jesus will the soul be saved from hell and damnation, there is also a "this-worldly" aspect to salvation. In becoming a "consecrated Christian" (in the words of the above sermon), the social and economic ills that befall a person will be overcome. As I was told many times by my Honduran evangelical friends, God's grace for eternal life manifests in blessings bestowed upon dedicated believers in this lifetime. Typical blessings such as economic success, healing, and family cohesion are evidence of an individual's dedication to God and his or her saved status. In particular, one's spiritual salvation will manifest in the alleviation of social and economic conditions that cause distress and suffering. In other words, salvation concerns both the soul and the body. In the neoliberal era in Latin America, a time when hunger, disease, and violence cause acute bodily suffering, evangelical religions have gained many new followers through promising a future end to worldly suffering through conversion and leading an austere moral life. By eschewing behaviors that are considered immoral and against God's will—such as drinking, dancing, and permissive sexual behavior—converting to an evangelical faith breaks from established social norms, signals to the larger community one's righteousness, and, in the process, transforms one's relationships with others in the community.

For example, Brusco (1993, 1995) describes how conversion to evangelical Protestantism by poorer women provides them with a moral foundation upon which to criticize men's destructive and immoral personal consumption (alcohol, prostitutes, maintenance of and gifts for other women) and reinforces moral household consumption. Mariz and Machado (1997) go so far to say that Pentecostalism "domesticates" men, integrating them into the domestic sphere (see also Flora 1976; Mariz 1998). In addition, because Pentecostals view women as more receptive to the Holy Spirit and as better faith healers than men, women gain symbolic power within a congregation (Chesnut 1997:99–102). Church involvement and attendance give women more freedom to leave their homes and take public roles as leaders (Brusco 1993:148), offer them expanded support networks to address domestic violence (Burdick 1993:107–115), and give them greater moral authority (Chesnut 1997:120–121). Overall, church involvement and belief in personal salvation offer women an opportunity to be active agents in directing their homes and communities.

The salvation promise of Pentecostalism is one of healing, both personal and social (Chesnut 1997). Pentecostal belief and practice integrate the fragments of believers' racial, gender, and class identities into a coherent, alternative set of social norms. The new norms (i.e., ethics) order Pentecostals' way of life as separate from the society in which they live. In areas of heightened state violence, such as Guatemala and Peru (Delgado 1998; Garrard-Burnett and Stoll 1993; Green 1993), conversion to Pentecostalism and other forms of evangelical Protestantism marks the believer as being apolitical, especially in areas where perceived "radical" Catholics involved in liberation theology are persecuted precisely for their political interpretation of social injustice. Evangelicals distance themselves from the political and social landscape, turning to God to save them from the violence around them. The supposedly "nonpolitical" Protestant faiths become a strategic resource for those hoping to escape the politically motivated violence against Catholics. As a separation from dominant society, conversion to Pentecostalism in contexts of civil war may provide practitioners with the spiritual resources to rebuke violence, as well as a community of believers to insulate them from its effects.

In El Progreso, as in other major cities in Honduras, Pentecostalism is also a resource for those young men and women seeking to escape everyday social violence. However, violence in Honduras is not limited to state-linked institutions such as the police or military but, in fact, is just as likely to come from youth-on-youth violence in the form of gang warfare. The politics of conversion, then, focus not on escaping persecution so much as on escaping the social and economic pressures that might lead youth to join gangs. Conversion is also a strategy for some young men to leave gang life. For other young men and women, Pentecostalism offers real and imagined security from possible physical harm in the form of violent threats, theft, and assaults. Conversion and membership offer youth a safe passage in their own and surrounding communities, a refuge from everyday violence, or, better said, a sanctuary that provides them with a protected status. Conversion creates a new social identity, but it is an identity that must be maintained over time.

Conversion: Maintaining a New State of Being in the World

Religious conversion is not an overnight event. Despite Austin's (1962) assertion that words can change states of being, saying the right phrase in the right context may alter one's status, but it does not maintain that status over time. There is a qualitative difference between performing a marriage ceremony by pronouncing "husband and wife" and christening a ship. Although both are done with words, the latter requires none of the minute social strategies drawn upon to maintain the status of the former. In much the same way, while confessing one's faith in Jesus in the Pentecostal tradition may signal that one has been "saved" from eternal suffering (much like baptism signals inclusion in a religious community and the celebration of one's first communion changes a Catholic's status from entry-level member to adult), it is a social category as much as a spiritual one. As a social category, conversion requires community acknowledgment of the new state of being. Conversion is much more a dialogue about faith and practice than a punctuated, one-time event.

In their treatment of evangelical intrusion and conversion in South Africa, the Comaroffs (1991) argue against employing the term *conversion* as a sociological category, in favor of examining how the converted manage their new identity. Conversion, they believe, reifies and solidifies the very fluid characteristics of "religious belief" into a single and homogenizing entity, thus overriding the ways in which individuals choose from a variety of signs and interpretations. They assert that "conversion" as a category indiscriminately combines "individual spiritual identity with cultural transformation" (Comaroff and Comaroff 1991:250–51). They warn that the two may not always be connected.

These caveats are useful in avoiding the pitfalls of using conversion as an analytic category, that is, conversion as some kind of objective change in status that is tied to numeric values and classificatory schemes. However, we must consider the poetics and politics involved with conversion for those who are engaged in the practice of convincing others to join a movement and those who contemplate joining. Although I am leery of placing too much weight on the concept of conversion, I believe it is impossible, given the sociocultural context of evangelical faiths in Latin America, to overlook the concept altogether. Conversion is a powerful heuristic that organizes much of the discourse and practice of evangelicalism generally, and Latin American Pentecostalism in particular.

I heard many conversion stories from Pentecostals in Colonia Belén and witnessed many actual conversions during church services and evangelizing campaigns. Indeed, not many church services went by without someone either converting or reconciling with God and the church. Typically at the end of the church sermon, the pastor or leader of the service will call out into the congregation, exhorting the attendees that someone there is being called by the Holy Spirit to come forward and accept Christ. The Holy Spirit may be the agent of change, but sometimes the Holy Spirit needs some assistance. Isabel, the youth coordinator at the Pentecostal church, explained to me this process concerning a recent youth evangelizing campaign.

> ISABEL: It isn't man that is going to change man, it is only God that can do so, only God can convince man to change, to make him see the need to change. So, preaching occurred and it is possible that the Word [of God] was planted, but it was necessary to confront the young man with his situation, with reality. And suddenly I felt, by the power of the Holy Spirit, I was told that there were three youths . . . and that these youths would not be able to leave there like that, and so I began to intervene, and I said, "There are three young men touched by the Word, the Word is planted [in them]." Many youths, out of fear, don't come to the front [of the church to convert]. . . . I felt so happy in this meeting, because I could see God's support, we could feel how God wanted to offer so much love to these young men, for there was a moment when I told the others, when I called to the other young men and women of the church to hug those young men who were there at the pulpit crying, and they came there and hugged them and prayed for them. This was to tell the others, "Give them love," because those young men lack love, it was to give them love, to hug them, to pray for them, to bless their lives and let them know that society might abandon them, but the church, in us, we will not abandon them, nor God. Much less God! Right? God is there to welcome all of those who may come to him.

For Isabel, the Holy Spirit was active in calling the young men forward to convert. As she described it, the seed had been planted in the young men, but that was not enough for them to overcome their fear. In this case, as these young men had been involved in a gang, Isabel explained that although the seed had been planted, the young men had yet to learn how to trust in God's protection. So, Isabel, also being directed by the Holy Spirit, called out to the congregation, drawing out from the attendees these young men. She intimates that all of her actions were directed by the Holy Spirit, from calling out to these young men to asking that the youth of the church come and pray over them. Yet the work of God could not be done without the support of the wider church community. Her explanation is an apt description of the double process of conversion: one's soul is saved when the Holy Spirit calls upon a person to confess and accept Christ, but it is the church that fosters the growth of the person after conversion.

Although conversion may receive a great deal of "public play" by the church and congregants as the defining moment upon which one's membership into a community of believers hinges, one's status as a *cristiano* depends more on day-to-day practices and community recognition. As the Comaroffs suggest for the Tswana converts, ". . . those marginal men and women drawn into the church soon realized that they had to accept, in no small measure, its methodical, rule-governed regime: to be seen to adopt, that is, the conventions of [the white missionaries]" (1991:247) Conversion, in other words, is but the beginning of a long process, and, as the sermon quoted at the opening of this chapter reminds us, it requires dedicated practice. Perhaps, like all identities, being a cristiano is contingent, being both an ascribed and attributed status. The contingent and emergent aspects of being a cristiano are most visible in the relationship between youth gangs and evangelical churches. Gangs and evangelical churches exist in an uneasy relationship, whereby young men involved in gangs are allowed to leave gang life via church participation. In the process, however, gang members view themselves as being the enforcers of God's will if an ex–gang member fails in his acceptance of Christ and does not behave as one who is saved.

The Interplay between Gangs and Evangelical Churches

Gang members, as well as others in the community, regard evangelical churches as a reforming institution, a viable resource for changing one's self-destructive behavior, owing to the churches' break from the ethics and practices of everyday working-class life. These religious ethics prohibit drinking, drug use, dancing, and sexual licentiousness, as well as require that public retribution of offenses be left in the hands of God. To a certain degree, they "domesticate" men by turning their behavior away from the values of a public street persona to the more private domestic sphere. The following excerpt from an interview with Arturo expresses the relationship between gang members and cristianos using an idiom of mutual respect that is predicated on cristianos' closer relationship to God:

> ARTURO: No, it's respect. You mess with a cristiano, it's like you're messing with God, and he who messes with God ends up losing everything, even life. So this is about respect. If a cristiano doesn't lack respect for you, you don't lack respect for him. But if a cristiano comes and he treats you like a son of a bitch, you hit him. Simple. You don't say anything to him. Hit him and that's all. This is the motto that we have for cristianos. But if a cristiano only goes walking by and only because he goes walking by and you come and say no, I don't like that cristiano, you're going to hit him for no reason. You have to respect them, because they are children of God. We're also children of God, but they're following the law of God. We don't. This is what happens, because this is about respect for cristianos. . . . We're all cristianos, but they live a better life because they worship God.

In Arturo's logic, cristianos, by virtue of "following the law of God," are due a respectful distance by others in the community. God's protection for cristianos derives from a superstitious belief on Arturo's (and other gang members') part that if they were to harm an innocent cristiano, God would seek revenge unto their death. However, if they judge that someone has been "unchristian-like" in their behavior toward them, gang members will not hesitate to be the enforcers of God's justice for not following his laws. Arturo is unwilling to remove gang members from the realm of Christendom, believing that all gang members are cristianos. The difference is in one's public appearance and the level of commitment. If cristianos follow God's laws—proscriptions against immoral behavior based on biblical interpretation—they are worthy of the deepest respect for leading a moral life.

Cristiano young men and women must demonstrate to gang members their devotion to their church. This includes semiotic markers of their status, such as the orderliness of their dress (long pants and shirts tucked in for young men, heeled shoes and knee-length dresses for young women), their ability to quote scripture and evangelize to members of the community, their length of involvement in the church, and their relationship with other cristianos in the neighborhood. If a cristiano young man is caught drinking alcohol, doing drugs, smoking, or dancing in public, his reputation is suspect. Such behavior indicates that the young man did not have a true commitment to the path of God, but instead turned to evangelical Christianity in an insincere effort to have the best of both worlds—protection of the church and ability to lead an immoral life.

Currently involved gang members, ex–gang members, and others in the community told me on numerous occasions that the only way for a young man to leave a gang, once involved, was to convert to an evangelical religion. I inadvertently touched on this in a conversation I had with Walter, himself an ex–gang member who had converted to Pentecostalism, about the recent murder of a gang member who I had been told had converted.

> WALTER: So this is a law that they have, if you don't serve El Barrio [the gang], than you serve El Colocho [the Curly-Haired One], Jesus Christ. So, this is it. This young man died because he did not, in truth, he did not serve the Lord, like, like the Lord Jesus Christ himself would have wanted. Instead, he went to indulge himself outside [of the church].
>
> JON: There are only two options?
>
> WALTER: There are only two options.
>
> JON: The gang or Jesus Christ?
>
> WALTER: Or Jesus Christ. Only two options. Well, Jesus Christ is a miracle, only a miracle for [those who wish to leave the gang], because if they leave [the gang, then the gang] kills them. They say that it is like a circle, the gang is like a circle. They say that there is a circle with fire all around it, and there is this circle. While you remain inside this circle you don't get burned, but if you stay, if you try to leave, you get burned. Like they all say, if he leaves, they kill him. But nothing more than, like I tell you, a miracle of God can take him out of this circle. That's how it happened to me.

Walter's comments point to more than just a sociological law concerning legitimate ways to leave the gang. Like others, Walter states that only God can extract a person from the "ring of fire" that is life in the gang. Like Arturo, Walter also points to the regulatory way in which others in the community continuously monitor one's behavior as a cristiano. Members of the community, including members of the young man's old gang, had seen him drinking and smoking marijuana in public. Purportedly, a member of the same gang as the victim was responsible for the murder in question. Walter did not question *who* monitored the young man's behavior (in this case, members of the victim's own gang) in deciding whether he had made a sincere change to Pentecostalism.

Rather, Walter merely indicated that the young man's behavior was not as God would have wanted and that for this reason he was murdered. Although the church may offer refuge, the refuge endures only as long as young men abide by the rules of public behavior that the church sanctions. If a young man fails to alter his behavior, then the decision is that of the gang members. They are the ones who judge whether a young man has sufficiently changed his behavior, whether he has demonstrated that he is a *cristiano de corazón,* a Pentecostal to the core. The miracle that Walter alludes to need not be direct intervention from God in a literal "saving" of a young man, although, as we shall see, there is this aspect of the miraculous that Pentecostals believe in as well. The miracle is what occurs in the transformation of one's behavior from violent gang member to active church member.

In a similar vein, Isabel emphasized that fear of one's own gang may be the very thing that prevents a member from leaving. It is implied that this fear arises from not trusting God, not giving in to God's desire for a member to leave the gang. If gang members were to submit themselves completely to the will of God, they would be secure in their new social position as cristianos, because there would be no mistaking them for their past identity.

ISABEL: For example, if a young man is from a gang, they say at times, "Well, I run the risk of danger if I leave the gang," right, because those that don't, those that stay in [the gang], they can very well do something to those who have left [the gang], to their family, taking revenge on their families. So, many of them, out of fear, they don't want to yield to what God wants in their life.

Reprisals are real enough and often the threat of harm can be a deterrent to leaving the gang. However, evangelical churches, through their recognized ability to provide a break with the norms of violence and addiction prevalent in gang life, are able to offer young men a promise of safety by requiring that they completely alter their old behaviors. Through the insisting on the existence of a direct, interventionist God, Pentecostalism also offers young men a theology of protection by God if, in the words of Isabel, they yield to God's will. Conversion offers safe passage out of the gang and into the mainstream community under the watchful eyes of God. Evangelical churches act as the intermediary between the gang and the community, with conversion as the catalyst to leaving, and the starting point for a new social identity.

Young men and women who have converted to Pentecostalism most often described their experience as being both product and process. Pentecostals express the product and process of conversion in spatial semantics, using the metaphors of arriving at the church and being on the path of God. For example, the pastor's sermon used both of these spatial metaphors in directing youth to the church as an alternative to violence and drugs. Thus, it may be fruitful to think of converting to Pentecostalism as entering into a new category of social person. Although the moment of transformation is signaled by a formal declaration of one's sins, the real work, as my Pentecostal friends would tell me, begins after public confession. After conversion, one must reorder one's social and spiritual life, as one's relationship with family, community, and God has now changed. In particular, conversion inscribes young men into a new social identity marked by a state of grace offered by God that is distinct from the "poisonous streets" where they live. In the discussion that follows, I weave the two phases of product and process together to understand the poetics and practice of these identities.

Conversion: Coming to the House of the Lord and Being on the Path of God

The momentary "product" of conversion, the changed state of being through which conversion creates a new relationship with God, is aptly described in spatial terms by Pentecostals as arriving at the house of the Lord and being on the path of God. The pastor, in his sermon, employs the metaphor of the house of the Lord for the church as the "resource" for families dealing with violent children. Later in the same sermon, he ties together being in the Lord's presence and being on the right path as a "priority" for youth. This is fitting in light of the social aspects of evangelical faiths, which, through active evangelizing, bring their vision of salvation to the larger society in the hope of curing social ills (Wilson 1997; Míguez 1998). This view is very different from the political and social activism in CEBs; instead of changing social structures to bring justice to an unjust world, for Pentecostals the conversion of individuals to accept the Holy Spirit provides the impetus for social change (Lancaster 1988:110–115). The more converts there are to Pentecostal standards of ethics, they believe, the more just the world will become. Indeed, conversion is part of God's plan; his call to the world is facilitated through evangelizing to others, but it is ultimately God who transforms nonbelievers. Feelings of anomie and social dislocation are overcome through involvement in Pentecostalism, offering converts feelings of security in a world that is profoundly insecure (Mariz 1994; Míguez 1998), both through participation in the church community and through God's protection.

Many young men and women explored the link between reaching spiritual salvation and the social context of youth violence in their conversations with me. In the following excerpt, Tina describes how she came to be a member of the church and, in her words, started on the "path of God."

TINA: Once, we had some friends and when they shot at them they killed one of them, and we, well, I felt that I had, I couldn't, I had no other option to save myself. The only option was God, because it was very sad, perhaps, seeing the people that one cares about most, what was happening to them. And it was a terrible day, and in the evening, we came to the church, and since then we are in the church, with challenges, struggles, but we go on.

JON: Tell me how, how this day was when they shot at . . .

TINA: Oh, this was a Sunday. We had come from a retreat, a fast here in the church. We left at like twelve, I think, and about one in the afternoon we were going to celebrate my brother's birthday, because he already went to church. And, then, a car was around, all mysterious, going up and down [the streets]. The car didn't have license plates. Not only that, this was in Fourth Street, and well, a cab driver arrived and told us to be very careful because there was a car without plates going around, and up there [in another neighborhood] they were putting mud [on the license plates], covering up the license plates. Well, then they warned all the young men not to go outside, and they, for being gawkers they wanted to figure out what was going on. They went to a friend's house, and when they left they said they were going to see what was happening. And when they came, there were three of them, and they shot one in the head, they shot at Lucas, and the other young man that is now, that's in a coma. But it was horrible, because I, I, yes, I was outside when I saw this, and I ran on the sidewalk from side to side, and I couldn't find the door to the house, and the door was open, and it was really sad. My mother exited running for the other side, she thought that they were going to kill her too. This was horrible, horrifying, horrifying, and this was the root of how I arrived on the path of the Lord.

Prior to this shooting, Tina had not been a serious member, like her younger brother, of the Pentecostal church. She would attend, visiting at her brother's suggestion, but had not made a formal declaration, a formal conversion. This drive-by shooting on their street was the violent catalyst that brought Tina and her mother to the church as formal members. The shooting proved to be the impetus for seeking the security offered by God in the form of the church, or, as Tina puts it, she had no other option to save herself.

The story of Tina's conversion is indicative of the strong relationship between personal salvation and social suffering. They came to the church, she states, implying that it was in the church that she and her family found security by appealing to God through conversion. Tina makes the distinction between attending church services, something she did prior to the shooting incident, and spiritually attending the house of God through formal conversion. In her comments, Tina indicates that a sense of safety, not solely formal membership, was the product of her conversion. Evangelical churches, invested as they are with a reputation of being "separate" from much of community life, build upon this reputation by presenting an image of safety and stability in an unstable and insecure social setting. A characteristic of evangelical Protestantism in Honduras is the emphasis that churches place on converting young men and women. The pastor who read from Leviticus 10:7 in the sermon quoted at the beginning of this chapter metaphorically highlights this protective feature of the church by suggesting that death will threaten those who leave the church: "'Do not leave the entrance to the Tent of Meeting or you will die, because the Lord's anointing oil is on you.' So they did as Moses said." His admonition to parents that followed the quoting of this Bible passage juxtaposes the holy ground of the church and that of the streets: "Parents, if you don't want your children to find themselves in gangs, in drugs, and in prostitution, be an example and come to Christ. . . . If you mothers no longer bear your sons being in drugs, in delinquency, search for life in Jesus." The church—as a physical location and as a body of believers—acts as a metonym for Christ. If, as I was told many times, Christ is the only way to reach salvation, joining the church is the only way to join him.

The pastor's rhetorical exploration of Leviticus 10:7 is dramatically—and literally—recreated in the following story told by gang member Arturo. The events he describes took place when he was considering leaving the gang by joining an evangelical church. Although ultimately Arturo did not leave the gang, his story demonstrates an almost literal recreation of the pastor's interpretation of Leviticus 10:7. As such, the story vividly points to the protective power of churches within the community.

> ARTURO: They [the gang] were in a meeting and it was my turn to go to this meeting that day, but that day they [the gang] told me that there was war [fighting between two rival gangs]. So I decided, my mother just died, I say, my mother just died what more do I want [in life]? I started thinking various things, but I don't know, it didn't give me anything to go to church that day. I came . . . so we went to [a nearby neighborhood]. We walked, me with a . . . I had a shotgun. I shot like three times. Afterwards my *carnalito* came and he told me, "Lend me the shotgun," and I took a chimba off another guy, and he carried the chimba. Like, twenty minutes later the police find us, and we come from up there, all of us running, some to one side, some to the other, but all the police come behind us. We say, "Run!" And so we run. When I come to the corner of the street where doña María lives, they fire two shots at me. They try to shoot me, but they couldn't hit me. When I come by, when I'm passing by like this by the corner where doña María lives, I spin around to see them, and I see that there is a church meeting. All at once I go in, and doña María says to me, "Sit here, sit here," and I stayed there, seated. I became surprised, because, I say, I was afraid, then, I didn't need to be doing these things, but I don't know, I didn't thi–think, I didn't think, and what I did think turned out bad for me. I only left running, I only left running. After, when I left the church meeting, the police had already gone . . .

Arturo had started out the day planning to go to the church. It was a time right after his mother had died of cancer, and he was reevaluating his involvement in the gang. However, the call to battle a rival gang had gone out, and Arturo decided that it made little difference whether he continued in the gang now that his mother had died. On his way back from the fight, as the police are chasing him and others from his gang, Arturo runs into the yard where the church meeting that he was going to attend is being held—at the house of doña María. In that moment, he escapes the captors and the shots that were being fired at him by the pursuing police. Doña María, by incorporating Arturo physically into the meeting and giving him a place within the circle of church members at her house, provides actual sanctuary in a moment of violence. By providing actual sanctuary, the church meeting also gives him a place to contemplate the state of his eternal soul in a moment when his life is in danger. When Arturo comments that, "I became surprised, because, I say, I was afraid, then, I didn't need to be doing these things," he expresses second thoughts about his involvement in the gang and what his future might hold.

Although not all evangelical churches seek to serve as a sanctuary for violent youth who wish to change their personal behavior, most of the evangelical churches that I encountered in working-class and working-poor neighborhoods in El Progreso did have ex–gang members among their congregants. At the very least, they were aware that other evangelical churches had become refuges for ex–gang members. As for the Pentecostal church in Colonia Belén where I spent the most time getting to know members, the church had a community reputation for evangelizing gang members. Although the majority of this evangelizing was done by other youth (ex–gang members or not), church leaders actively endorsed these actions in their sermons, at church events, and, through what could best be described as community outreach. Focus on youth, on violent and drug-addicted young men in particular, was a prime part of all evangelizing campaigns that I witnessed. The underlying rationale is that for positive social change to occur, young men and women must first change their own personal behavior via the church. Orvin, a Honduran Pentecostal pastor, expressed this idea in the following way:

> ORVIN: Honduras is truly living the chaos of, of a lot of violence, of a lot of gangs, but we are seeing how God is truly working, because today we are seeing that Honduras is being invaded by the gospel, right. Today we watched here in [the colonia] where we are constructing the new church building, I heard the loud shots of the gang members, fighting within range. There, there you could not walk during the day, let's not even talk about at night. But now we are seeing, truly, that many have come to Jesus Christ because the Word of God here in Honduras is being spread all over the place.

Notice the contrast between the violence of the community (the gang members' shoot-out) and the potential for safety in the community through the spread of the gospel. By describing the community in the imperfect past tense ("there you could not walk during the day, let's not even talk about the night"), he describes a state of being that contrasts with the current process of evangelization. For Orvin the process of change in the community is one in which people come to Christ (and hence safety) *through* the place of the church. In his comment, Orvin collapses both the physical location of the church in the neighborhood and the ideological space that the church holds as an agent of social change. His comment parallels the distinction between going to church and actual conversion.

Young men's desire to find a safe place through participation in the church is made even more explicit in the following passage by Enrique, a twenty-five-year-old Pentecostal who has worked extensively in evangelizing gang members.

ENRIQUE: Many of them [young men] arrive with the huge burden that their life has been lost. They come to God's feet seeking a true refuge, not a false refuge like the devil gives them, presents to them. Because they have felt that the only true way to live is to search for God. They have seen that the Devil has come to kill, to steal, to rob, to fool many people. And blessed be the Lord that he has opened their eyes. And they have seen that all the evil that they committed before has been an abomination in the eyes of God. And they have sought God out, not out of personal interest, not an interest of the flesh, but for a spiritual interest. It has been God who has touched their lives through the Word, through biblical readings. And today they feel attracted not to a man, not to a person, not to a woman, but to God, because he is the only one these days that can change the mentality of these people [meaning gang members].

One day I was so moved, and they made me want to cry, because one of them said, "What a psychologist would try to do in my life for fourteen years, God has done to me in one day. I couldn't leave the drugs, I couldn't leave my former life, I couldn't stop thinking about evil things, but one day I came and I gave myself to the Lord. The Lord touched my life, washed my spirit and my soul, and since that day I am a new person." This has attracted them [to the church], because they have seen that the hand of God moves powerfully not only in the church, but in all the places where God is praised and served. And knowing this is an incentive in their lives. Maybe some of them took the lives of other people, maybe when they consumed drugs they felt like a caged animal, like some tiny bird enclosed in a cage that has nowhere to leave, and that their life was in danger, because being in the gang runs the danger of dying. . . . Now the night is not a common night, it is not just any kind of night. It is a dangerous night, because constantly you hear, whatever corner here in the street, shots, deaths, assassinations, young women being raped, and it [the church] practically comes to be like a refuge, that, I sincerely say, I believe with all my heart, that very few people succeed in finding. And blessed be God that they have succeeded in finding it, not in us, not in people, but in God, in his house.

Enrique's comments suggest a dichotomy between the "true refuge" of the church and the "false refuge" of the Devil. In other words, there are two options: taking refuge in a corrupt world, a world of violence and drugs, symbolized as being owned by the Devil, or taking refuge in the church, the "house of God." This echoes Walter's statement that there are only two options for the gang member—the gang and the church. And, as in Orvin's comment, there is a conflation of the church as a physical location and the church as a metaphysical place wherein one finds the strength to change self-destructive behavior.

An emphasis on the transformative powers of God is also evident. Enrique reports that one ex–gang member had told him, "The Lord touched my life, washed my spirit and my soul, and since that day I am a new person." Expressed through a common metaphor of cleansing, the statement highlights the sense of rebirth—becoming a new creature—that is central to Pentecostalism's promise of salvation from social ills through conversion. One's soul is cleansed of all impurities at the moment of conversion, but only through practicing continued upright moral behaviors does the soul remain untainted. Changing status from a gang member to a "new person" requires the elimination of certain behaviors—doing drugs, murdering, fighting, and so forth—yet this change in behavior requires the presence of *being in* a church. Their status changes precisely by seeking sanctuary in the church. Like the political refugees in Cunningham's (1995) and Coutin's (1993) ethnographies, these young men experience a change in status that places them betwixt and between their old state of being in the gang and the everyday violence they encounter on the street.

Enrique points to the extralocal power that integration into a church has in terms of changing one's status socially as well as personally. By *extralocal,* I mean that the refuge of the church extends beyond the walls of the building and beyond meeting as a congregation. When discussing the appeal to gang members of joining a church, Enrique states, "This has attracted them [to the church] because they have seen that the hand of God moves powerfully not only in the church, but in all the places where God is praised and served." The protective power of God, which is where the church derives its power to offer sanctuary (Cunningham 1995), extends to believers outside of church walls as long as they continue to praise and serve him. The onus of protection ultimately lies on the young men. Belief in God is not enough to save one from harm; one must also continuously demonstrate this belief through one's actions in the world, or, in the words of the sermon quoted at the beginning of this chapter, through demonstrating one's dedication to the Lord. The local explanation for why evil befalls people, even evangelical church members, is that they were not living in the morally right way. Witness Sergio's description, in the opening chapter, of Títere's murder. Sergio states that Títere had incurred God's wrath because Títere asserted that "he was going to stay in the streets. And God proved him right. As [Títere] said, so God made it so, 'if he [Títere] was born for the streets, he's going to die in the streets.'" In other words, Títere, by not choosing God, chose death, dramatically enacted by his being gunned down in front of his own house. God's protective path is available to young men only if they demonstrate that they are saved from violence through their actions. If they should "fall" or have a relapse in violence or alcohol use or drug addiction, they would be accused of "playing with God" by gang members and open themselves up for violent retribution. Gangs judge who has authentically become a Christian, based on an individual's public performance of being a cristiano.

Sanctuary and the Protective Path of God

The extralocal power of sanctuary offered by evangelical churches to young men derives from their ability to demonstrate effectively their status as dedicated cristianos. By proving they are on the path of God, young men are able to invoke God's protection from harm. As Arturo commented above, gangs are reluctant to cross cristianos for fear that God will exercise retributive justice. Thus, sanctuary is a portable possession that must be invoked during discursive interactions between Pentecostal young men and those who threaten their safety. For them, sanctuary exists everywhere as long as they remain on the "path of God."

To better illustrate the belief that the protective state of God travels with the true believer, we must look at instances in which young men have invoked their special status as beneficiaries of God's protection.

During my fieldwork, I collected a number of stories by Pentecostal young men, including some who were ex–gang members and some who were not, who maintained that their social status as Pentecostals helped them avoid possible violent assaults and thefts by gang youth. Most of these stories recounted events that occurred in the neighborhood. This is notable because, while young men credit divine intervention in giving them safe passage and a lack of fear in their social mobility, their moments of grace were also contingent upon their assailants recognizing them as Pentecostals. Most Pentecostals of varying ages and genders credited the presence of God in their lives when a potentially bad situation turned out for the better. However, only young men recounted stories in which they were repeatedly saved from street violence and protected in moving about the city at all times of the day because of an interventionist God. These stories are part of a genre in which young men reinforce the protective status of the church as sanctuary by describing the ways in which they continue to be saved by divine grace, even after initial conversion.

Consider, for example, the following story, as recounted by Davíd.

DAVÍD: One time, they [gang members] assaulted me and stole my shoes. I was going from the church, we were praying all night until like two in the morning. And we were going to drop off my aunt, and out of nowhere some young men appeared. And they told us, "Take off your shoes!" So, so with dread and fear, right, that they were going to do something to us, because one of them was pointing a gun at us, they take our shoes. We went barefoot! Well, so in that moment in which they told us "Go, go, take off your shoes," then we tell them "No, we're cristianos." We tell them, "Why are you doing this to us?" Then, "No, take off your shoes. Don't say anything. Take off your shoes." So we take off our shoes. Later, we came walking with two more members of the church. When we came, we came here by way of the parish [building]. They [the gang members] leave from the side of the creek, and they throw us our shoes, and they say to us, "Take your shoes," he tells us. And so, we go to fetch them. They returned them to us, he says, "Because you never denied that you were cristianos." They told us like that. So they gave our shoes back. We were so happy to have our shoes, right. . . . But, so, the truth is, that I wasn't afraid, because I knew that God was with me and the Bible says that if God is with us, who is against us? Well, God instills courage in us, he places courage and strength in us.

David's encounter with local gang members could have ended disastrously. When I later questioned Sergio, the gang member who had assaulted David on this occasion (the two had since become friends and members of the same church), he told me that he had purposely set an ambush for David's cousin, who owed Sergio money, with the intention of doing him bodily harm. Sergio commented earnestly, "If it had been [David's cousin] and not David that night, he would be dead. I would have killed him I was so angry [over the money]." David's insistence on his identity as a Pentecostal was the deciding factor that made Sergio aware that he had the wrong guy, as it was often pointed out to me how similar David and his cousin look and sound. David, in his version of events, stressed his continued belief in God's protective power as being, in fact, the very thing that saved him. He may have been afraid at the moment of the assault, but looking back on it, he claimed to have been unafraid because God was on his side, something that he drew from a close reading of the Bible.

Invoking immunity to assaults by gang members by explicitly proclaiming oneself as a Pentecostal is also clear in the following two stories taken from my fieldnotes. Both involve Pentecostal young men who were once gang members themselves.

Fieldnotes, May 9, 2002. Last night, two different gang members near the water tank assaulted Lucas. They demanded that he give up his bike—giving him the shakedown. Lucas' response: "*Tranquilo, tranquilo.* I haven't messed with you. I'm cristiano, man." One, according to Lucas, was obviously jacked up on drugs and wouldn't pay him any heed, pulling out a huge chimba and getting ready to try it out on Lucas. The other one, though, getting a good look at Lucas in the darkness, says, "Hey you [*vos*], I know this one. It's true loco, he's a cristiano, loco. Let's leave him, okay, let's let him go. We don't mess with cristianos, man." And so Lucas was reluctantly allowed to go.

Fieldnotes, March 12, 2002. Walter launched into a great story about how his cousin's bike had been stolen by gang members recently. He was convinced by his cousin to go and ask for it back, and so went to talk to an old friend of his who is still involved in the 18th Street Gang. This friend said not to worry, he'd take care of it, and he'd come and talk to Walter in the afternoon. When he arrives, they go to see El Jefe of the gang.

Walter says, "And the Jefe says to my friend, '*¿Qué pedo jomi? ¿Quién es esto loco?*'" [What's with this homie, who is this dude?]

"No, he's nothing, he's not one of us, he's a cristiano."

The whole time Walter is there, he is real careful to use not his friend's *apodo* [gang name], but his real name, in a strategic move to disassociate himself from the gang. The Jefe, in reprimanding the gang member who stole the bike, says, "You can't steal from El Colocho [Jesus]. When you rob a cristiano, you rob El Colocho."

In the first story, Lucas avoids potential violence by proclaiming himself a cristiano. His assertion is successful, however, only after he is recognized as such by one of his assailants. In the second story, Walter's identity as being outside of the gang world is confirmed by his old friend to the *jefe* of the gang and reinforced through two linguistic strategies. First, Walter is careful not to address his friend by his gang name. Second, when El Jefe at first wants to ascribe to Walter the status of loco, a social category used by gang members to describe themselves, Walter's friend immediately rectifies this by reinscribing Walter as a member of a distinct category, as a cristiano. In both cases, the liminal status of Lucas and Walter as outside of community violence is contingent upon their ability to define themselves as members of evangelical churches. They reside beyond the enactment of violence because of their association with God. This is made explicit when Walter quotes the speech of El Jefe that draws a metonymic association of Pentecostals with Jesus: "You can't steal from El Colocho. When you rob a cristiano, you rob El Colocho." Gangs don't want to mess with a cristiano, for fear of calling down God's wrath.

Young Pentecostal men are not always able to escape assaults by gang members in their community, however. In the following example, seventeen-year-old Manuel relates how he and his best friend, Tomás, were robbed and assaulted walking home late one night.

MANUEL: Once we were coming from a [church] vigil with brother Tomás, and we were going to drop off a member of the church, a leader of the church. And two individuals, when we arrived at Belén, right there at the entrance of Belén, two guys from the 18th Street Gang asked us for money. They took our dough and they took our money. And after this, they asked us for our clothes, and they left us in our underwear, and they beat us up with our very own belts. They beat us up! It was really ugly.

JON: And what did you do?

MANUEL: I ran with Tomás. And I was in boxers, because I don't use bikini briefs, and Tomás does use bikini briefs, and they left him in only the briefs and me in boxers. And I ran and we ran for the pastor's house, and he wasn't there, only the pastor's wife. And as I was in boxers, with shame, but I asked for a towel to cover Tomás because he was walking around sexier than I, let's say, because he was in briefs. And there she healed us, she put some stuff on us, because they busted me open here in this part of the ear, they busted me open with the belt, they hit us. They gave me two big hits in the shoulder, and they hit Tomás in the nose, in the face. They made him bleed a lot. But they've already died. I always had this trust that said, says the word of God, that with your own eyes you will see the reward of the impious and with my own eyes I saw how they came to nothing. Once I was going to [church] group, it was my turn to go to [the neighborhood] Tres de Marzo, the group in [the neighborhood] Los Robles. I was going to Los Robles, and I saw how they killed one of them there in Belén's soccer field. There I saw how they killed one of them, and the other I saw without hands, without either hand, and I said: "Lord, sincerely, what you say is true, with my own eyes I was going to see their reward, the reward of the evildoers."

Even though Manuel and Tomás failed to be protected from the assault, Manuel recast this failure in terms of divine social justice. Although he was still assaulted, he knew that his gang-member assailants were going to get theirs in the end. In a twist on Weber's promise of salvation, Manuel was assured that he would receive compensation for the act of violence perpetrated against him and his friend. Weber originally conceived that the promise of salvation could be a radical form of rebellion against the dominant social classes, rather than an ideology to justify intraclass warfare (Lancaster 1988; Weber 1993). Here, however, young men from the same economic class are pitted against each other, and the outcomes are not the social liberation that Weber had in mind. The ideology of salvation, even though used as a means to reach out to gang members, is also used to explain their eventual demise for not heeding the call to change their lives. Parallel to the real violence inflicted by gang members is this symbolic violence of a vengeful God who exacts retribution on behalf of his believers.

The above encounters between Pentecostal young men and gang members make evident that Pentecostal young men invoke the protective symbolic power of the church in concrete ways. They, and other young men, extend the refuge offered by evangelical churches in two ways. First, Pentecostal young men are able to negotiate their way out of potentially harmful situations through the implicit social contract between gang youth and non-gang youth. This negotiation is predicated on Pentecostal young men positively demonstrating their "Pentecostalness" to others. Only through the continued practice of their identities is such a guarantee of safety possible.

Second, in these encounters we are able to see the externalization of a belief in the protective powers of God offered by conversion. These young men have marked out a social space for themselves in the materialization of their new social status as Pentecostals. This social space is invoked only in those encounters in which their safety is called into question. The sanctuary of the "church" (as a building, as a community) becomes a device with which they can travel safely. In many ways, Basso's conclusions regarding the sacred landscapes of the Western Apache hold true for these Pentecostal young men: "Thus transformed, landscapes and the places that fill them become tools for the imagination, expressive means for accomplishing verbal deeds, and also, of course, eminently portable possessions to which individuals can maintain deep and abiding attachments, regardless of where they travel" (1996:75).

While Basso's argument concerns the historical and mythical relationships Western Apaches hold with the land on which they live, for Pentecostal young men in Honduras a no less "real" connection exists between themselves and their churches. Instead of a relationship to the land that becomes uprooted and resituated through linguistic practice, a spatial relationship becomes "unhoused" from the community in which it resides and is made portable through conversion. Conversion reorients the believer socially and spatially. These young men are able to invoke their status as cristianos and their deep attachments to God's protection wherever they go in the community.

As a result, Pentecostal young men actually become *more* mobile than the "domesticated" men Brusco (1995) and Mariz and Machado (1997) have described among Colombian and Brazilian evangelicals. Their lack of fear, derived from carrying their sanctuary with them, affords them the ability to move freely about the community during day or night, something that would normally have placed them in danger.

Their very liminality is their key to mobility. Unlike the Central American refugees offered sanctuary by U.S. churches in the 1980s and 1990s, who found that they became immobile due to reliance on sponsoring churches (Coutin 1993), Pentecostal young men who receive a type of social amnesty through the sanctuary offered by conversion continue to play a public role in the community. They exist beyond the reach of community violence, but within the church, and, as they would express it, the church resides within them.

Conclusion

For Pentecostals, becoming a member of the church means leaving all other paths to be on the path of God. This is the path of reforming behavior, of changing one's attitude, one's position in social life. When I asked Sara, a seventeen-year-old Pentecostal group leader, how she would advise some of the recent ex–gang members of her group, she used the spatial metaphor of two paths as a heuristic to order right and wrong:

> SARA: Well, my advice would be that, maybe this young man, if he uses drugs, what I could counsel him is that he should first of all separate himself from this path, he should leave to one side those things which are going to bring him nothing good, because the Word says that he who walks in evil finishes in evil. So, he should separate himself from this path and truly start with a new life, being another person, a useful person in society, because at least within society these people—these young gang members—are . . . how would you say it? . . . a threat to society. So, that he might be something useful for society and go to a church, because this is my job, speaking to this person of the Word, and if he really wants a change in his life, go searching for God because he knows that God is the only way out. . . . God is what is going to change him. Maybe he can speak the Word to these people, but if their heart is harder than stone, the Word is not going to enter them. Meanwhile, if he is always speaking the Word to them and searching for God, God is going to do the work. Maybe not in an instant, maybe many years from now, but the Lord is always going to do the work.

Her advice is for those young men to leave behind one path and take up another. By switching from being a threat to something useful in society, and thus by altering their social spaces, the young men, over time, will arrive at that place where God is in them, God is moving within them, doing his work through them. For Sara, only by opening one's heart to the Word can this fundamental change in one's being happen. In many ways, she is saying that only by internalizing the message of conversion is one able to change his or her social position.

In his ethnography of crack sellers in East Harlem, Philippe Bourgois provides insight into the ways in which those most marginal to society eventually become agents of their own marginalization, because of the structural inequalities that they confront on a daily basis. As he concludes, "I was forced to recognize . . . the brutal dynamic whereby tender victims internalize the social structures that dominate them, to the point that they eventually take charge of administering their own mutual self-destruction" (1996:264–265). Socialization, in his example, went hand in hand with self-destruction, with little hope of changing the social order of things. Although I do not wish to be overly optimistic about the power of religion as a transformative social agent, I have offered here a counterexample whereby some equally socially marginalized young men have internalized a competing set of social structures (and the related social relationships that accompany them) that may sometimes "save" them from everyday violence.

Conversion to an evangelical faith radically respatializes its members as distinct from the community at large. In the process, Pentecostals place themselves in two distinct spaces, in the house of God and on the path of God. These spaces metaphorically remove young men from harm's way into the protective space of sanctuary. By employing these spatial metaphors, the poetics of conversion create new social spaces and hence new social beings—young men who are not implicated in delinquent behavior.

Young men who convert to leave gangs use conversion as a strategy to overcome, in some way, the effects of institutional forms of violence as embodied by gangs and, to a lesser degree, state institutions. They extend the Pentecostal spatial metaphors of the house of God and the path of God that are available to them as converts to provide protective space in their interactions with other youth. It is a creative and unintended use of Pentecostal ideology that young men put into practice for themselves. Conversion is a resource that is available to some young men who can counter the spatial logic of the streets with the spatial logic of sanctuary. In this way, the institutional character of organized religion battles against the institution of street gangs.

Conclusion
Taking on Violence

"Come On Guys, Violence Is Bad"

José Luis was a fanatic about his muscles and self-conscious about his slight stature. Not a bulky young man, he was "ripped" and undeniably strong. This didn't stop him from crying to Sergio and myself, "I need to put some weight on. Look how scrawny I am." In the yard across from his parents' house, cluttered with scrap metal from his father's repair shop, the three of us lifted weights. José Luis and his older brother fabricated dumbbells by filling various sizes of tin cans with cement and connecting them with metal rebar. The result was the most extensive set of home gym equipment in Belén.

José Luis and Sergio were afire when it came to lifting, doing large numbers of multiple sets in quick succession without breaking a sweat. Before they had decided to convert to Pentecostalism, Tupac or Control Machete would have set the tone to lift by, the rap music's steady beats providing the pulse. They have replaced rap with a borrowed worn-out cassette of Pentecostal hymns, mostly an upbeat and steady rhythm with lyrics that proclaim them "warriors for Christ."

I couldn't keep up with them and sweated profusely in the late afternoon heat. José Luis had me on the bench doing dumbbell flys. Carlitos, who turned thirteen during the year I had been living in the neighborhood, was on his afternoon rounds selling peeled oranges out of a plastic bucket. It was his way of making some cash, using the resources from his grandparents' orange trees. I was desperately in need of some sort of break from José Luis's workout regime. Seeing Carlitos pass by the shop, I called out to him for three oranges.

Carlitos was, as most of the neighborhood would have agreed in calling him, *malcriadísimo*—totally lacking in the fundamentals of social etiquette. He picked fights for no other reason than to boost his own self-esteem, he swore and tried in general to act "big." He would attempt not just to imitate the behavior of older young men in the neighborhood, but to surpass them. He sneaked drinks of beer and cigarettes. And street violence fascinated him. He knew the names of all the gang members around Belén and even fancied himself as being "connected" to them.

As Carlitos approached us, coming up the slight incline from the street, he dropped the bucket of oranges and grabbed at the waistband of his jean shorts, reaching under his shirt to pull out a gun. I didn't realize it was plastic until after he aimed at Sergio and pretended to shoot. The gun, a magnum .357, was almost a caricature of itself, because Carlitos was so out of proportion for such a large weapon: the barrel was as long as his forearm.

Sergio didn't flinch. He seized the barrel of the gun with his left hand. Yanking it toward him, he wrenched it from Carlitos's hand while hooking his right arm around Carlitos's neck. "You idiot!" Sergio hissed. "That's not how you do it." Sergio roughly placed the barrel of the gun to Carlitos's temple. "Like this. This is how you do it." After a tense minute, tense even though we knew the gun was plastic, Sergio shoved Carlitos out of the way and examined the gun.

José Luis, as if to defuse the situation by treating it as merely all in good fun, said in a mocking tone, "Come on guys, violence is bad." Sergio didn't hear him. Throwing the toy into the street, he said to José Luis, "That's like the one you had, isn't it?" Carlitos went running after the gun.

The exchange between Sergio and Carlitos frightened me. At one level, it encapsulated my greatest fears that violence is indeed cyclical and that there is no breaking that cycle. Even though social violence must be transmitted in order to be perpetuated, watching violent acts instructs one in the ways of being violent. Carlitos may have been play-acting, but play-acting is a short remove from the real thing. At a more personal level, watching Sergio's behavior made me realize just how much violence was a part of his life, even corporeally. He had made great changes in the short months that I knew him, altering his physical comportment, curtailing his social involvement with many of his old friends, and professing religious belief with the intensity of a neophyte convert. Yet something of his old life remained. Indeed, with this and other interactions, I began to question how much Sergio *had* really changed. Was he just performing for me and others in the community? Other ex–gang members in the church, those who had been out for more then a year, seemed to have accepted wholeheartedly their new identity. But was

Sergio just using conversion as a temporary reprieve? It was naive of me to believe that a person could transform that much in such a short amount of time. How much of the public persona Sergio portrayed was out of desperation and fear?

I do not have an answer to that. It would be impossible to speculate on Sergio's motives. As close as we had become, and as much as he confided in me, Sergio also kept his cards close to his chest. I do know that drug addiction is not easy to overcome, and that there were occasions when Sergio went on crack benders. With each one, he would confess to me how awful it made him feel that the drug owned and controlled him. As far as I knew, though, he had not returned to thieving or causing bodily harm to anyone. However, watching him and Carlitos, I did not doubt that the power of guns was just as addictive as drugs.

I knew of other young men who had been out of gang life for two or three years. When they were willing to talk to me about the initial decision to leave the gang, it was always with stories of physical and emotional struggles. Yes, leaving behind their drug addictions was difficult, they would tell me, but so was constantly proving to others that they had truly changed. This was perhaps even more difficult, because young men could not easily leave their social milieu. They were stuck having to leave their old reputation behind, something that followed them wherever they went in the neighborhood.

Sergio's brother, Julio, urged him to convert to Pentecostalism. Julio had converted a couple of years before and relied on the network of church members as a surrogate family, especially since Julio and Sergio's parents had died. Sergio had distanced himself from his extended family because of his gang involvement. Aunts and uncles refused to offer him a place to stay at night and even denied him food. I am unsure what Julio ultimately said that convinced Sergio to convert to Pentecostalism. Sergio had become increasingly isolated from his family, and many of his longtime gang friends, including El Títere, had been murdered. His brother and the Pentecostal church were the only alternative to the support that the gang offered.

I had met Sergio before he converted. At the time, I did not openly encourage him to leave the gang. When I discovered he had converted, I immediately felt I had to show him that I supported his decision. I also knew it was important for him to be seen in public with me. Many of the Pentecostal young men who helped guide Sergio through the first months of leaving the gang also self-consciously spent time in public

with him. It was as if we were displaying to the community that we supported Sergio and that the community needed to treat him respectfully.
We demonstrated that Sergio was no longer a gang member, through
our interactions with him, the way we greeted him on the streets, and
our willingness to offer him food and share soda with him. In essence,
we helped give Sergio a new social life.

Sergio and I spent a lot of time together. I must admit that I wanted
him to succeed so badly that I found myself checking up on him. Two
months after Sergio converted, Julio left to migrate illegally to the United
States. Although the two had talked it over, it was an emotional blow to
Sergio. He became depressed and turned back to crack. I had grown to
admire Sergio and valued our friendship. Against my better judgment, I
increased the amount of time we hung out together, as I was afraid that
once Julio left, Sergio would lose much of his support. My last months
in Honduras I spent riding the emotional roller coaster of Sergio's life.
By the time I left, I wondered if Sergio would go back to the gang. Had he
found enough support to not return to his former life? In the last month
of research, when Sergio expressed doubts about staying in the Pentecostal church, I told him outright I did not care if he stuck with religion.
I only cared that he not go back to the gang. Sergio laughed bitterly and
told me he had no other choice until his brother could get him to the
United States. I did not bring the topic up again. He knew his options
far better than I did.

Making Do in an Environment of Violence

All young men I knew had internalized a certain amount of street savvy.
Whether they had been a part of a gang or not, they had their own ideas
about how gangs and gang violence operate. They also had a good understanding of the response of the state and local institutions to violence.
Moreover, all were familiar with the lack of economic opportunities for
youth. Indeed, young men lived and created the intimate knowledge as
to the causes and effects of youth violence. Any response to the logical
underpinnings of the system that destroys young lives had to develop
with that system in mind. In other words, in a violent environment,
social actors, regardless of the risks involved, will craft social mechanisms to cope with their surroundings and maneuver through the violence of everyday life. These mechanisms do not necessarily transform
the violence around them; they just make violence more manageable.

It is with this in mind that young men and women are left to take on violence, either through confrontation with everyday violence or appropriation of violent means.

Collectively, youth manage their social environments in creative ways and are coproducers of the meanings that circulate in society. Although rarely in positions of power, because of their age, gender, or economic resources, youth are social actors who act and react to the world around them in novel ways. They are more than vessels of socialization. Youth instruct each other, and their actions inform the responses of others in their community. Panter-Brick (2002) suggests that one way to honor the creative aspects of living is to shift the scholarly discussion about youth to the examination of resilience in responding to stress and adverse situations. Resilience sets the research agenda to examine the practices that young people use to negotiate everyday life. "It is wrong to assume that vulnerability or protection lies in the variable (e.g., social support) per se, rather than in the active role taken by individuals under adversity: Resilience is a reflection of an individual's agency" (Panter-Brick 2002:163). Focusing on resilience allows us to see the creative ways in which individuals resist and recapitulate structural conditions in their lives. Resilience relies on innovation and adaptation to the social environment to produce innovative reactions in adverse situations.

I consider resilience to be a primary form of what de Certeau aptly terms "the art of making do" (1984:xv). The art of making do is the myriad of creative tactics that the popular classes use to consume and re-present cultural forms. In the process of appropriating the meanings and practices of various institutions for their own purposes, youth create new ways of understanding their lives and demonstrate their resilience in the face of violence. In this book, I have presented a number of tactics youth employ to neutralize the psychological and physical effects of urban violence in their lives, of making do with what is available to them in order to go on with their lives.

Some aspects of everyday life exert unswerving force on youth. The structural violence of neoliberal economic measures, high unemployment, and diminished educational resources for youth restrict the types of responses youth can make. State policies that implement neoliberal economic reforms disinvest funds and interest in the lives of youth. Relying on neoliberal reforms to boost the national economy increases the social attenuation and lack of opportunities for young men and women in areas of education, job training, and formal-sector employment.

What little safety net there had been for youth has disappeared. Lack of opportunities for young men translates into increased joblessness and apparent aimlessness. Finding themselves more and more outside of traditional institutions of support such as school, work, and family, young men are also outside of acceptable society. This places them in harm's way. Out-of-bounds, they are emblematic of the ills befalling Honduran society (crime, a failing economy, corruption) and are set up as scapegoats.

Gangs are one alternative for youth who feel the absence of institutional structures in their lives. Gangs provide an alternative set of supports that replace family and state institutions. Yet gangs also require an immense loyalty in return. Gangs obligate their members to commit acts of murder to demonstrate allegiance. This includes violence that regulates group cohesion, and adhesion to its rules. If a member attempts to leave gang life without going through the appropriate channels, his own gang marks him for death. As alternative institutions, gangs foster only the most tenuous form of sociability among their members, bound together by violence and drug use. Tattooing and graffiti are two practices used by gang members to instill loyalty to the group. They are the primary ways in which interpersonal relationships are mediated and reinforced in gang life. Despite their dangerous consequences, gun violence and gangs have a gritty glamour and propose an alluring alternative identity. Gang nicknames, tattoos, and graffiti transform outcast kids into a community force to be reckoned with. Boys such as Carlitos romanticize the empowering aspect of gang life, recognizing it as a quick avenue to forms of respect not found elsewhere.

While some young men may join gangs as one tactic to cope with violence, others join religious movements. Youth link themselves to both Catholic and evangelical Christian churches, acquiring these institutions' various resources and repositioning themselves within their shelter, however temporarily. Churches provide guidelines for behavior in the form of popular theology. Although their approaches differ with denomination and local membership, churches act as competing institutions, setting themselves in opposition to the state and gangs.

The Catholic Church provides the most visible "replacement" programs for youth. These supplement, and sometimes supplant, those offered by the state and include education, health, and recreation programs. At the community level, the Catholic Church, at least in El Progreso, organizes youth to be a visible and beneficial force in their community through collective social action. While the prevailing image of youth in Honduras is one of violent gang members, this action on behalf of the church balances, to a small degree, the image of youth.

Evangelical churches, especially Pentecostal churches, approach youth from another perspective. They encourage young men and women to separate themselves from the "evils of the world," which include vice and violence. Individual salvation, propagated through evangelizing to others, is said to bring about collective change. If enough youth convert and stop their wicked ways, then the nation will change. Such an attitude places the onus back on the individual. Young men may be able to find sanctuary from violence within the church, yet this sanctuary is contingent upon their continued dedication to their faith. Political economic strictures, which limit one's opportunity and exacerbate violence, challenge one's faith. As Pentecostals told me many times, poverty is not evidence of an unjust distribution of wealth and abuse of power. The poor remain poor because of their lack of faith in God.

Violence has long-term effects on the organization of social ties, fostering changes in the approach to social relations. In this sense, violence is productive, both breeding more violence, as in the above narrative concerning Carlitos, and demanding creative solutions to mediate the effects. In other words, where there is pernicious violence, there must exist ways to cope. Otherwise, the effects of violence would destroy the human will altogether. I have offered evidence for resilience in the face of adversity.

Although unable to alter the macroeconomic forces in their lives, youth make choices in how they deal with structural and gun violence. They choose the resources that they feel best enable them to make do, whether joining a church or a gang, spending time on the street or inside their homes, doing drugs, or working any available job. The power of gang and religious institutions is that they can partially shield youth from urban violence, if not economic injustice. Yet these institutions also benefit from the existence of urban violence, because they gain membership as a result of it. The institutions that have developed as a result of social attenuation are the very same that benefit from a continuation of these conditions.

Youth twist the social meanings of institutions to create new approaches to violence in their communities. Manipulating the codes and interpretation of doctrine, youth may challenge both institutions and dominant understandings of youth violence. This is most clearly demonstrated in the differing understandings between youth and religious institutions of neighborhood space. With an emphasis on managing the quality of their social relationships in space, as opposed to the places where violence occurs, young men and women organize their own particular understanding of neighborhood space. Using narratives, which anticipate the types of social relationships that can occur in particular locales, youth order and name places as safe or dangerous.

The young men of Colonia Belén are intimately familiar with violence. It is a part of the very fabric of their upbringing, as they came of age during the U.S. military presence in Honduras because of the Contra War in Nicaragua and the increase in crime and availability of guns brought on by the Peace Accords in El Salvador. They also spent their formative years during the initial implementation of neoliberal economic reforms. Those who were born in the late 1970s and early 1980s have known nothing other than diminishing opportunities for advancement and increasing consumer demands. They have always been in the thick of physical and economic brutality. The collective malaise that youth express is a result of their double bind. Not only must they witness the murder of their peers, they also live everyday their own social death of not being able to rise above their station in life (see Wolseth 2008). Indeed, many see that they will not even meet the standard of living of their parents.

There is currently very little political space open for Honduran youth to express their grief and discontent. The threat of murder has diminished the public space available to them, truncating a formerly vibrant street life, much less the ability for collective political action. Youth participation in the political process is limited, unless it is their contact with a faulty judicial system bent on incarceration, or a police and military aimed at elimination of youth from public arenas. Church organizations offer the only viable, positively sanctioned alternative for young men and women to be present in public. They also provide, for some youth, the space in which to reflect on the situation of their country and the economic and gun violence they experience. Other spaces of reflection are rare for working-class and working-poor youth.

Currently, there is no conceivable end to youth violence in Honduras. Short of transnational migration, the likelihood of a better future for my friends is grim. Violence works in a cyclical pattern because no alternative intervenes. Carlitos felt the lure of violence, the empowerment that gangs and guns provide. Sergio, despite claiming he had broken with his violent past, still fell back, effortlessly, on the knowledge he had acquired while in the gang. The fluid way in which he wrenched the gun from Carlitos and earnestly went through the motions of executing him was matched by the nostalgia he felt for guns and his past. The slippage was only momentary, but it demonstrated just how close to the surface his past was. Even though Sergio and other young men take the steps to leave a violent lifestyle, violence is a pervasive part of the social landscape. There is, in essence, no escape, just degrees of involvement.

Years have passed since I lived in Colonia Belén. I am not the same wet-behind-the-ears, twenty-six-year-old budding ethnographer. With the perspective of time I have matured to see the missteps I made in my professional and interpersonal relationships in the field. In particular, I think of Sergio. His story remains clouded. Accounts of his fate by friends of mine in the neighborhood are by turns tragic and obscure. His brother, Julio, made it to the United States, aided by an uncle in Connecticut whom he had not seen for a decade. Within months of Julio leaving El Progreso, I too left. I wish I could say our parting was on good terms, but I knew Sergio well enough by then to see the resentment and abandonment in the rigid posture and curt way we shook hands. The other young men in the church offered him temporary support, but when Sergio's behavior started to place them at risk, they too abandoned him. Sergio went back to smoking crack. Soon, in order to fuel his consumption, he turned back to the gang with greater verve. It took time for Julio to become established in his new life. His unfulfilled promises to send for Sergio strained their already tumultuous relationship. I can imagine Sergio becoming despondent, desperate for something to lift him out of his current life.

The last I heard of Sergio was almost two and a half years after having left Colonia Belén. On a visit to New York City, I met up with Walter, who had crossed illegally into the United States a year before. He lived in a dingy basement apartment in Brooklyn with a Salvadoran family who had taken him in. It was a dislocating experience for both of us to see each other in this new context. Sitting next to each other on the worn-out tan sofa in the darkened living room, Walter even commented, "Geez, Jon, imagine it, here I am in your country. Who'd have thought that we would see each other here?" Walter was in much better contact with the neighborhood than I had been. We spent the hours catching up. He offered updates of the people we knew in common. I was surprised at how many of the young men were now spread across the United States, working in construction or in chicken processing plants. Davíd was married to Amalia now. Manuel was expecting his second child. Tomás lived in Baton Rouge. Lucas had made several attempts to cross the border, being detained and deported each time.

As we went through the list of people we knew, my mind kept returning to Sergio. Walter hadn't brought him up, and I was reluctant to ask, still feeling the bite of shame and guilt. Finally, as it was nearing time for me to leave, I mustered the gumption to ask. I took a swig from the glass of Pepsi and said, "And Sergio, Walter. What happened to Sergio?"

"Jon," Walter began but then paused and repeated, "Jon, things didn't go well for Sergio after you left. He stayed with the church for a while but went back to his old life. He fell hard. He attacked a bus full of passengers near La Lima, Jon. He killed innocent people. He was taken by the police, and no one has ever seen him again."

That was as much detail as Walter was going to offer me. He may not have known much more. I had heard enough to confirm my anxieties over Sergio's condition. Walter must have seen the crestfallen look on my face, the numb shock of surprise my eyes registered. "No, Jon, if Sergio had wanted to change for real, he would have. Look at me, or Tomás, or Lucas. We all got out of the gang. We changed our life. It is no one's fault, Jon. Sergio didn't call on God to strengthen him, to give him resolve. Only God can be your anchor in this world."

Walter's words didn't offer much solace, no matter what truth they contained about individual resilience in the face of adversity and the will to change. Sometimes we need help to find our center, to stop the world from spinning too fast. I stared out an empty window on the subway back to Manhattan, thought of Sergio, and cried.

Appendix of Names

Amalia: Amalia is twenty-two years old. She attends university classes at night, works from her mother's home as a hairdresser, and is a group leader for her Pentecostal church.

Arturo: Arturo is twenty-two years old. He has been a member of the 18th Street Gang since he was fifteen. Although he started high school, he dropped out after his father left for the United States and his mother passed away from cancer. He lives with his aunt.

Carolina: Carolina is twenty years old. Originally from the city of Comayagua, she arrived in El Progeso at the age of eighteen to work in a maquila and help a cousin take care of her infant son. A practicing Catholic, Carolina attends the youth group when she is able.

Chago: Chago is twenty-eight years old. He works in the informal sector as a middleman providing goods to mom-and-pop shops throughout El Progreso. He is a prominent figure in Belén's Catholic church, serving as youth group facilitator, leading church services when the priest is absent, and sitting on a number of parish-wide committees.

Davíd: Seventeen-year-old Davíd is in his last year of high school and hopes to study journalism in university. He has been a Pentecostal for more than four years and is a leader of his own growth group. He converted without his mother and sister (Tina) and eventually brought them to the church as well. His father has been in the United States for the past ten years.

Delfina: At thirteen years old, Delfina is the youngest member of the Catholic youth group. In addition to attending secondary school, she works part-time for the Catholic youth radio station in town. She and two other young women have a weekly radio show for children.

Diego: Diego is a twenty-one-year-old. He, his wife, and young son live in his mother's house, along with his seven siblings. Diego occasionally works in construction or in his brother's furniture repair shop. He attends Catholic church services and youth group regularly.

Eber: Twenty-two-year-old Eber studies computers and business at a private university in San Pedro Sula. His parents own a number of small businesses, including several taxicabs and buses. Eber began attending Catholic youth group when invited by a member of his weekend soccer team.

Elizabeth: Elizabeth is sixteen years old and is still in high school. Her parents have seen that she and her three older siblings continue in school. Her family is very involved in the Catholic Church. All three of her siblings have attended youth group at one time or another.

El Títere: El Títere, whose gang name means "The Puppet," was murdered outside his grandmother's house at the age of nineteen. He had been a member of the 18th Street Gang and Sergio's best friend.

Enrique: Enrique is a group leader for the Pentecostal church. Married and with three kids, he works at a maquila. Enrique sees it as his duty to evangelize to gang youth in his community. He is twenty-five years old.

Fernando: Fernando works as a diesel mechanic. Twenty years old and unmarried, he lives with his family and helps pay his younger siblings' school fees. He attends Catholic services and youth group when his work allows it.

Isabel: In her late twenties, Isabel is the youth coordinator for the Pentecostal church. She is married with two children. Her husband has lived in the United States for over seven years, sending money back regularly.

Joaquín: Joaquín is a twenty-five-year-old Pentecostal. He is an ex–gang member who claims responsibility for bringing the 18th Street Gang from Los Angeles to El Progreso when the Immigration and Naturalization Service deported him as an illegal alien. He is married and has two children.

José Luis: Twenty-year-old José Luis chose self-imposed "house arrest" for a year while he decided whether he wanted to leave the 18th Street Gang. He eventually converted to Pentecostalism.

Lucas: Lucas, twenty years old, converted to Pentecostalism after his now-defunct gang, Los Wanderers 13, became absorbed in inter-neighborhood gang warfare. He works odd jobs in the informal sector from time to time. Lucas's relationship with his family is strained, and he divides his time sleeping in his uncle's house and on the floor of the church.

Manuel: Eighteen-year-old Manuel had been a member of one of the first local neighborhood gangs, Los Axis, at a very young age. He converted to Pentecostalism when he was fifteen. As with Lucas, Manuel's relationship with his father is strained, and he divides his residence between the homes of his older siblings.

Marcos: Marcos, twenty-three years old, is a member of the Catholic youth group, although he does not attend Catholic services. He works at his uncle's machine shop in San Pedro Sula and lives with his parents in Belén.

Martín: Martín lives with his sister's family. He has worked off and on for the past six years at a variety of maquilas throughout Honduras. He is twenty-six years old, attends Catholic services regularly, and occasionally attends youth group.

Orvin: Orvin, in his early thirties, is an assistant pastor in the Pentecostal church. He and his wife work in the Pepsi plant in town. They have three children.

Pepe: Pepe, seventeen years old, attends a private Catholic trade school, where he is studying car repair. He represents Belén's Catholic youth group at the parish level.

Roberto: Seventeen-year-old Roberto left school because his family could not afford to send him to high school. He works periodically in retail shops in San Pedro Sula and El Progreso. He hopes to follow his father to the United States, where the man works in a large poultry processing plant. He attends Catholic Church services and youth group on a regular basis.

Sara: Sara, seventeen years old, is in her last year of a combined high school and secretary school program. She plans on working as an office assistant during the day and attending public university in the evening. She converted to Pentecostalism four years earlier and is currently a group leader.

Sergio: Sergio is an eighteen-year-old ex–gang member. He entered the gang at the age of thirteen, after the deaths of his parents from AIDS. He recently converted to Pentecostalism in hopes of leaving the gang.

Teresa: Teresa, nineteen years old, is in her first year of study at the university, focusing on business. When not busy with school, she is an active participant in the Catholic church, volunteering to visit the infirm of her congregation. She also attends youth group regularly.

Tina: Nineteen-year-old Tina is in her first year at the university, where she is studying business management. She is a group leader for the Pentecostal church and also a part of the church's music ministry.

Victoria: Victoria, twenty-three, married Chago in 2001, after a long courtship. They met each other in Catholic youth group. Victoria studies law at the university in San Pedro Sula.

Walter: Twenty-year-old Walter has been a Pentecostal for three years. Before converting, he was part of a local gang, a precursor to the gang 18. He is a group leader for his church.

Notes

Chapter 1

1. All personal names are pseudonyms.

2. Colonia Belén is a pseudonym for the neighborhood where I conducted fieldwork.

Chapter 2

1. In many of these discussions, claims to public space for new social movements were one visible way of moving into the public sphere (see, for example, the articles in Alvarez, Dagnino, and Escobar 1998).

2. Low (2000) draws a parallel between public spaces and democratic politics in her study of the plaza as a public space and cultured place in Costa Rica. Work on the Mothers and Grandmothers of Plaza de Mayo in Argentina also highlights the political implications of claiming public space. Schirmer asserts that the Mothers break "the binary spatial boundaries of private and public" and in so doing upset the state's ordering of a public space by making visible what the state wanted to keep hidden—the disappearance of supposed political dissidents" (1994:215). In both examples, users define the public space of the plaza as openly political, a place where a conversation with and about power occurs.

3. For a history of gang formation in Honduras, see Castro and Carranza 2001. This practice is not unique to Honduras. It appears to be a feature of Chicano and Latino gangs in general, one derived most likely from Los Angeles, where, in the early years of gang formation, gangs truly were a felt extension of the neighborhood in which the members lived (see Moore 1978; Phillips 1999; Vigil 1988, 2002, 2003). Gangs assumed the name of their neighborhood. However, with the spread and mobility of gangs, the correlation between gang name and neighborhood name no longer always exists. Members of the 18th Street Gang in Belén held the name of a street and neighborhood located in Los Angeles, a place only one of the members I talked to had ever lived in. Even the clique name was derived from an adjacent neighborhood, and not from Belén. Yet the practice of calling the gang by the general term for neighborhood points to the strong identification that members have between their local manifestation of the gang and the place where they reside.

4. Both *mara* and *pandilla* are generic terms used in journalism and everyday use by average Hondurans to talk about gangs. The terms are used indiscriminately and are interchangeable. However, when used by gang members themselves, the significance of each term as a way of designating the group becomes apparent in the local politics of gangs. *Mara* is used only by members of the Mara Salvatrucha (MS-13) gang as a general group descriptor; members of the 18th Street Gang use *pandilla*. It is a grave insult, as I found out inadvertently, to describe the 18th Street Gang as a *mara*.

5. This would be what Phillips identifies as "hitting up" and "roll call" graffiti—an affirmative annunciation of the gang's presence in the area (1999:118).

6. See chapters 4 and 5 for more detail on their distinct approaches toward, and resources offered to, youth.

Chapter 3

1. I was told by several current and ex–gang members that such written documents existed and were in circulation, although I never saw them myself. The tension between the agency evoked by the phrase "we all have the word" and a set of formal laws was glossed over by several of my informants. I believe what ultimately is of more value is a gang member's ability to speak with authority drawn from experience.

2. The process for gang members is akin to the effect that tattooing had on Samoan young men, whose tattoos signified the passing from young child into the status of adult warrior such that "young Samoans were enmeshed in a bodily practice which assured the coalescence of glory and submission, practical subjection represented as a net gain in honour and autonomy" (Gell 1993:58).

Chapter 4

1. See, for example, Mainwaring 1986 for Brazil, Berryman (1986, 1994) for El Salvador, and Dodson and O'Shaughnessy 1990 and Mulligan 1991 for Nicaragua.

2. Interestingly enough, neither Eber nor Marcos mentioned Honduras's long colonial and neocolonial exploitation as a possible root cause of violence.

References

Acland, Charles R.
1995   *Youth, Murder, Spectacle: The Cultural Politics of "Youth in Crisis."* Boulder, CO: Westview Press.

Adorno, Sérgio
2002   Youth Crime in São Paulo: Myths, Images, and Facts. In *Citizens of Fear: Urban Violence in Latin America,* ed. Susana Rotker, Pp. 102–116. New Brunswick, NJ: Rutgers University Press.

Alvarez, Sonia, Evelina Dagnino, and Arturo Escobar, eds.
1998   *Cultures of Politics, Politics of Culture: Re-Visioning Latin American Social Movements.* Boulder, CO: Westview Press.

Austin, John
1962   *How to Do Things with Words.* Oxford, UK: Clarendon Press.

Basso, Keith
1996   *Wisdom Sits in Places: Landscape and Language among the Western Apache.* Albuquerque: University of New Mexico Press.

Berryman, Phillip
1986   El Salvador: From Evangelization to Insurrection. In *Religion and Political Conflict in Latin America,* ed. Daniel H. Levine, Pp. 58–78. Chapel Hill: University of North Carolina Press.
1994   *Stubborn Hope: Religion, Politics, and Revolution in Central America.* New York: Orbis Books–The New Press.
1996   *Religion in the Megacity: Catholic and Protestant Portraits from Latin America.* Maryknoll, NY: Orbis Books.

Bourgois, Philippe
1996   *In Search of Respect: Selling Crack in El Barrio.* Cambridge: Cambridge University Press.

Brusco, Elizabeth
1993   The Reformation of Machismo: Asceticism and Masculinity among Colombian Evangelicals. In *Rethinking Protestantism in Latin America,* ed. Garrard-Burnett and Stoll, Pp. 143-158. Philadelphia: Temple University Press.
1995   *The Reformation of Machismo: Evangelical Conversion and Gender in Colombia.* Austin: University of Texas Press.

Bucholtz, Mary

2002   Youth and Cultural Practice. *Annual Review of Anthropology* 31: 525–552.

Burdick, John

1993   *Looking for God in Brazil: The Progressive Catholic Church in Urban Brazil's Religious Arena.* Berkeley: University of California Press.

Caldeira, Teresa P. R.

2000   *City of Walls: Crime, Segregation, and Citizenship in São Paulo.* Berkeley: University of California Press.

Campbell, Duncan

2003   Hundreds in Central America Are the Victims of "Social Cleansing." *Guardian,* May 29, 2003.

Castellanos, Julieta

2000   *Honduras: Armamentismo y violencia.* Tegucigalpa, Honduras: Fundación Arias para la Paz y el Progreso Humano.

Castro, Misael, and Marlon Carranza

2001   Las Maras en Honduras. In *Maras y pandillas en Centroamérica,* ed. Ricardo Falla, Pp. 221–332. Managua: UCA Publicaciones.

Chesnut, R. Andrew

1997   *Born Again in Brazil: The Pentecostal Boom and the Pathogens of Poverty.* New Brunswick, NJ: Rutgers University Press.

Cintron, Ralph

1997   *Angel's Town:* Chero *Ways, Gang Life, and Rhetorics of the Everyday.* Boston: Beacon Press.

Cohen, Stan

1972   *Folk Devils and Moral Panics: The Creation of Mods and Rockers.* Oxford: Blackwell.

Comaroff, Jean, and John Comaroff

1991   *Of Revelation and Revolution: Christianity, Colonialism, and Consciousness in South Africa.* Chicago: University of Chicago Press.

Conquergood, Dwight

1994   Homeboys and Hoods: Gang Communication and Cultural Space. In *Group Communication in Context: Studies of Natural Groups,* ed. Lawrence R. Frey, Pp. 23–56. Hillsdale, NJ: Lawrence Erlbaum Associates.

Coutin, Susan Bibler

1993   *The Culture of Protest: Religious Activism and the U.S. Sanctuary Movement.* Boulder, CO: Westview Press.

Cunningham, Hilary

1995   *God and Caesar at the Rio Grande: Sanctuary and the Politics of Religion.* Minneapolis: University of Minnesota Press.

de Certeau, Michel

1984   *The Practice of Everyday Life.* Berkeley: University of California Press.

Delgado, Manuela Cantón

1998   *Bautizados en fuego: Protestantes, discursos de conversión y política en Guatemala (1989–1993)*. La Antigua, Guatemala: Centro de Investigaciones Regionales de Mesoamérica.

Dodson, Michael, and Laura Nuzzi O'Shaughnessy

1990   *Nicaragua's Other Revolution: Religious Faith and Political Struggle*. Chapel Hill: University of North Carolina Press.

Durkheim, Emile

1995   *The Elementary Forms of Religious Life*. New York: Free Press.

Euraque, Darío

1996   *Reinterpreting the Banana Republic: Region and State in Honduras, 1870–1972*. Chapel Hill: University of North Carolina Press.

Flora, Cornelia Butler

1976   *Pentecostalism in Colombia: Baptism by Fire and Spirit*. Rutherford, NJ: Fairleigh Dickinson University Press.

Garrard-Burnett, Virginia, and David Stoll, eds.

1993   *Rethinking Protestantism in Latin America*. Philadelphia: Temple University Press.

Geertz, Clifford

1995   *After the Fact: Two Countries, Four Decades, One Anthropologist*. Cambridge: Harvard University Press.

Gell, Alfred

1993   *Wrapping in Images: Tattooing in Polynesia*. Oxford: Clarendon Press.

Gill, Anthony

1998   *Rendering unto Caesar: The Catholic Church and the State in Latin America*. Chicago: University of Chicago Press.

Girón, Carlos Enrique

2002   27 mil hondureños han muerto violentemente desde 1994. *Diario La Prensa*, July 8, 2002: 4–5.

Godnick, William, Robert Muggah, and Camilla Wasznick

2002   Stray Bullets: The Impact of Small Arms Misuse in Central America. Occasional Paper No. 5. Geneva: Small Arms Survey, Graduate Institute of International and Development Studies.

Green, Linda

1993   Shifting Affiliations: Mayan Widows and *Evangélicos* in Guatemala. In *Rethinking Protestantism in Latin America*, ed. Garrard-Burnett and Stoll, Pp. 159–179. Philadelphia, PA: Temple University Press.

Harris, Bruce

1997   *Informe de tortura a niños de la calle en Guatemala y Honduras*. San José, Costa Rica: Casa Alianza.

Hernández, Alcides, Mario Posas, and Julieta Castellanos
2000   *Gobernabilidad democrática y seguridad ciudadana en Centroamérica: El caso de Honduras.* Tegucigalpa: Centro de Documentación de Honduras (CEDOH).

Hewitt, W. E.
1991   *Base Christian Communities and Social Change in Brazil.* Lincoln: University of Nebraska Press.

Holston, James
1989   *The Modernist City: An Anthropological Critique of Brasília.* Chicago: University of Chicago Press.

Krauskopf, Dina
1998   Juventud y empleo en América Central a mediados de los 90. In *América Central en los noventa: Problemas de juventud,* ed. Carlos Ramos, Pp. 13–46. San Salvador: FLACSO Programa El Salvador.

LaFeber, Walter
1993   *Inevitable Revolutions: The United States in Central America.* New York: W. W. Norton.

Lancaster, Roger N.
1988   *Thanks to God and the Revolution: Popular Religion and Class Consciousness in the New Nicaragua.* New York: Columbia University Press.

Lanza, Leo Valladares
2002   *Informe especial sobre muertes violenta de niños, niñas y adolescentes en Honduras.* Tegucigalpa: Comisionado Nacional de los Derechos Humanos.

Lanza, Leo Valladares, and Susan C. Peacock
2000   In Search of Hidden Truths: An Interim Report on Declassification by the National Commissioner for Human Rights in Honduras. http://www.gwu.edu/~nsarchiv/latin_america/honduras/hidden_truths/hidden.htm (last accessed March 5, 2010).

Lefebvre, Henri
1991   *The Production of Space.* Oxford: Blackwell.

Lehmann, David
1996   *Struggle for the Spirit: Religious Transformation and Popular Culture in Brazil and Latin America.* Cambridge: Polity Press.

LeoGrande, William
1998   *Our Own Backyard: The United States in Central America, 1977–1992.* Chapel Hill: University of North Carolina Press.

Levine, Daniel H.
1990   Popular Groups, Popular Culture, and Popular Religion. *Comparative Studies in Society and History* 32 (4): 718–764.
1994   Authority in Church and Society: Latin American Models. In *The Roman Catholic Church in Latin America,* ed. Jorge Domínguez, Pp. 189–216. New York: Garland.

Low, Setha M.

1992   Symbolic Ties That Bind: Place Attachment in the Plaza. In *Place Attachment,* eds. Irwin Altman and Setha Low, Pp. 165–185. New York: Plenum Press.

2000   *On the Plaza: The Politics of Public Space and Culture.* Austin: University of Texas Press.

Low, Setha M., and Irwin Altman

1992   Place Attachment: A Conceptual Inquiry. In *Place Attachment,* ed. Altman and Low, Pp. 1–12. New York: Plenum Press.

Maciel, Creuza

1990   Grassroots Communities: A New Way of Being and Living as Church. In *Born of the Poor: The Latin American Church since Medellín,* ed. Edward Cleary, Pp. 99–103. Notre Dame, IN: University of Notre Dame Press.

Mainwaring, Scott

1986   Brazil: The Catholic Church and the Popular Movement in Nova Iguaçu, 1974–1985. In *Religion and Political Conflict in Latin America,* ed. Daniel H. Levine, Pp. 124–155. Chapel Hill: University of North Carolina Press.

Malkki, Liisa, and Emily Martin

2003   Children and the Gendered Politics of Globalization: In Remembrance of Sharon Stephens. *American Ethnologist* 30: 216–224.

Mariz, Cecília Loreto

1994   *Coping with Poverty: Pentecostals and Christian Base Communities in Brazil.* Philadelphia: Temple University Press.

1998   Deliverance and Ethics: An Analysis of the Discourse of Pentecostals Who Have Recovered from Alcoholism. In *More than Opium,* ed. Barbara Boudewijnse, André Droogers, and Frans Kamsteeg, Pp. 203–224. Lanham, MD: Scarecrow Press.

Mariz, Cecília Loreto, and Maria das Dores Campos Machado

1997   Pentecostalism and Women in Brazil. In *Power, Politics, and Pentecostals in Latin America,* ed. Edward L. Cleary and Hannah Stewart-Gambino, Pp. 41–54. Boulder, CO: Westview Press.

Massey, Doreen

1994   *Space, Place, and Gender.* Minneapolis: University of Minnesota Press.

Mentore, George

2005   *Of Passionate Curves and Desirable Cadences: Themes on Waiwai Social Being.* Lincoln: University of Nebraska Press.

Merry, Sally Engle

1981   *Urban Danger: Life in a Neighborhood of Strangers.* Philadelphia: Temple University Press.

Míguez, Daniel

1998   The Modern, the Magic, and the Ludic: The Pentecostal View toward an Insecure Life, an Argentine Case. In *More than Opium,* ed. Barbara

Boudewijnse, André Droogers, and Frans Kamsteeg, Pp. 35–52. Lanham, MD: Scarecrow Press.

Moore, Joan
1978   *Homeboys: Gangs, Drugs, and Prison in the Barrios of Los Angeles.* Philadelphia: Temple University Press.

Morris, James
1984   *Honduras: Caudillo Politics and Military Rulers.* Boulder, CO: Westview Press.

Moser, Caroline, and Dennis Rodgers
2005   Change, Violence and Insecurity in Non-Conflict Situations. Working Paper #245. London: Overseas Development Institute.

Mulligan, Joseph E.
1991   *The Nicaraguan Church and the Revolution.* Kansas City, MO: Sheed and Ward.

Municipalidad de El Progreso
1998   *El Progreso: Población y desarrollo.* El Progreso, Honduras: Unidad de Investigación y Estadística Social.

Panter-Brick, Catherine
2002   Street Children, Human Rights, and Public Health: A Critique and Future Directions. *Annual Review of Anthropology* 31: 147–171.

Phillips, Susan
1999   *Wallbangin': Graffiti and Gangs in L.A.* Chicago: University of Chicago Press.

Pine, Adrienne
2008   *Working Hard, Drinking Hard: On Violence and Survival in Honduras.* Berkeley: Unversity of California Press.

Programa de las Naciones Unidas para el Desarrollo (PNUD)
1999   *Informe sobre desarrollo humano, Honduras 1999.* Tegucigalpa, Honduras: Programa de las Naciones Unidas para el Desarrollo.

Riaño-Alcalá, Pilar
2002   Remembering Place: Memory and Violence in Medellín, Colombia. *Journal of Latin American Anthropology* 7 (1): 276–309.

Rodgers, Dennis
2007   Slum Wars of the 21st Century: The New Geography of Conflict in Central America. Crisis States Research Centre Working Papers Series 2, no. 10. London: DESTIN.

Rodgers, Dennis, Robert Muggah, and Chris Stevenson
2008   Gangs of Central America: Causes, Costs, and Interventions. Occasional Paper no. 23. Geneva: Small Arms Survey, Graduate Institute of International and Development Studies.

Rodman, Margaret
1993   Beyond Built Form and Culture in the Anthropological Study of Residential Community Spaces. In *The Cultural Meaning of Urban Spaces,*

ed. Robert Rotenberg and Gary McDonogh, Pp. 123–138. Westport, CT: Bergin and Garvey.

Rotenberg, Robert
1993   Introduction. In *The Cultural Meaning of Urban Space,* ed. Robert Rotenberg and Gary McDonogh, Pp. xi–xix. Westport, CT: Bergin and Garvey.

Rotker, Susan
2002   Cities Written by Violence: An Introduction. In *Citizens of Fear: Urban Violence in Latin America,* ed. Rotker, Pp. 7–22. New Brunswick, NJ: Rutgers University Press.

Ruddick, Susan
1998   Modernism and Resistance: How "Homeless" Youth Sub-Cultures Make a Difference. In *Cool Places,* ed. Skelton and Valentine, Pp. 343–360. London: Routledge.

Ruhl, J. Mark
2000   Honduras: The Limits of Democracy. In *Latin American Politics and Development,* ed. Howard J. Wiarda and Harvey F. Kline, Pp. 512–526. Boulder, CO: Westview Press.

Scheper-Hughes, Nancy, and Carolyn Sargent, eds.
1998   *Small Wars: The Cultural Politics of Childhood.* Berkeley: University of California Press.

Schirmer, Jennifer
1994   The Claiming of Space and the Body Politic within National Security States: The Plaza de Mayo Madres and the Greenham Common Women. In *Remapping Memory: The Politics of Time Space,* ed. Jonathan Boyarin, Pp. 185–220. Minneapolis: University of Minnesota Press.

Schulz, Donald, and Deborah Sundloff Schulz
1994   *The United States, Honduras, and the Crisis in Central America.* Boulder, CO: Westview Press.

Schutte, Ofelia
1993   *Cultural Identity and Social Liberation in Latin American Thought.* Albany: State University Press of New York.

Smith, Christian
1991   *The Emergence of Liberation Theology: Radical Religion and Social Movement Theory.* Chicago: University of Chicago Press.

Stephens, Sharon
1995a   *Children and the Politics of Culture.* Princeton, NJ: Princeton University Press.
1995b   Introduction: Children and the Politics of Culture in "Late Capitalism." In *Children and the Politics of Culture,* ed. Stephens, Pp. 3–48. Princeton, NJ: Princeton University Press.

Torres, Carlos Alberto

1992 *The Church, Society, and Hegemony: A Critical Sociology of Religion in Latin America.* Westport, CT: Praeger.

Tuan, Yi-Fu

1979 *Landscapes of Fear.* New York, NY: Pantheon Press.

Turner, Terence

1980 The Social Skin. In *Not Work Alone: A Cross-Cultural View of Activities Superfluous to Survival,* ed. Jeremy Cherfas and Roger Lewin, Pp. 112–140. Beverly Hills, CA: Sage.

1979 *Landscapes of Fear.* New York: Pantheon Books.

Umanzor, Sergio

2002 150 mil pandilleros han sembrando el terror en Centroamérica. *Diario La Prensa,* February 8, 2002: 30–31.

Urban, Greg

1996 *Metaphysical Communities: The Interplay of the Senses and the Intellect.* Austin: University of Texas Press.

Vásquez, Manuel A.

1998 *The Brazilian Popular Church and the Crisis of Modernity.* Cambridge: Cambridge University Press.

Vigil, James Diego

1988 Group Processes and Street Identity: Adolescent Chicano Gang Members. *Ethos* 16 (4): 421–445.

2002 *A Rainbow of Gangs: Street Cultures in the Mega-City.* Austin: University of Texas Press.

2003 Urban Violence and Street Gangs. *Annual Review of Anthropology* 32: 225–42.

Weber, Max

1993 *The Sociology of Religion.* Boston: Beacon Press.

Wilson, Everett

1997 Guatemalan Pentecostals: Something of Their Own. In *Power, Politics, and Pentecostals in Latin America,* ed. Cleary and Stewart-Gambino, Pp. 139–162. Boulder, CO: Westview Press.

Wolseth, Jon

2008 Everyday Violence and the Persistence of Grief: Wandering and Loss among Honduran Youths. *Journal of Latin American and Caribbean Anthropology* 13 (2): 311–335.

Wolseth, Jon, and Florence Babb

2008 Introduction: The Cultural Politics of Youth in Latin America. *Latin American Perspectives* 35 (4): 3–14.

World Health Organization (WHO)

2002 *World Report on Violence and Health.* Geneva: World Health Organization.

Index

agency, 8, 15, 133, 144n1
apodos. See 18th Street Gang: nick-
    names
Archbishop Romero, 81

base ecclesiastical communities: char-
    acteristics of, 72; and neoliberalism,
    89–93; political role of, 81–82, 89,
    100–101, 114; and practice of faith,
    75, 80–81, 83, 85, 99, 105; youth
    groups modeled after, 76, 98
blood brother, 25, 53, 56–57, 68, 70.
    See also carnal

carnal, 8, 25, 34, 53–59, 62, 67–71, 117.
    See also blood brother
Catholic: belief in forgiveness, 25, 75,
    79, 87, 98–101; competition with
    Evangelical churches, 9; faith,
    23, 25, 45, 83, 88; participation in
    community, 25, 75, 78, 80, 82, 87,
    93, 98, 105; political involvement,
    107; relationship with God, 84–85;
    social services, 7, 76, 134. *See also*
    base ecclesiastical communities;
    Catholic youth group; solidarity
Catholic Church: institutional
    changes in, 80. *See also* base ecclesi-
    astical communities
Catholic youth group: and gangs,
    25, 30, 54, 89, 93, 96–97, 101; meet-
    ings, 21, 75–83, 88, 90, 93, 105;
    modeled after base ecclesiastical

communities, 76, 98. *See also* base
    ecclesiastical communities; Catho-
    lic; solidarity
CEB. *See* base ecclesiastical
    communities
CELAM. *See* Latin American Bishops'
    Conference
Central American armed conflicts,
    12, 47
citizen insecurity, 7, 10
comunidad de base (CEB). *See* base
    ecclesiastical communities
conversion: as means to leave gang, 3,
    26, 73, 107, 113; to overcome social
    problems, 21, 105–106, 114, 119–120;
    for protection from violence, 105,
    107, 119, 122–128; and separation
    from community life, 128; and
    social identity, 107–108, 110, 114;
    and social suffering, 116
crack addiction, 50, 52, 131–132, 137
crime: and distrust, 86; and El
    Progreso, 17; and unemployment,
    91–93, 134
cristianos: relationship to gangs, 4,
    110–113, 121–124, 126

de Certeau, Michel, 8, 53–55, 59, 68, 133
discourse: and community, 33, 54, 68,
    78–79; and crime, 29; and morality,
    79, 82; and sanctuary, 82, 108; and
    violence, 29–31, 36, 46–47
Durkheim, Emile, 9, 79

18th Street Gang: assault by, 58, 66, 123–125; and Colonia Belén, 39–40, 123–124, 140–144; control over space, 8, 24, 27, 39; as El Barrio, 25, 39–40, 112; graffiti, 8, 25, 30, 39–41, 65–69; nicknames, 8, 39–41, 54, 65–67; as *pandilla*, 40, 144n4; as social institution, 39, 41–42, 52–59, 71, 128, 134–135; tattoos, 2, 8, 25, 64–65

El Barrio, 25, 40, 112

El Progreso: Catholic Church in, 76, 134; conducting fieldwork in, xi, 15; economic production in, 16–17; gang activity in, 54, 57, 65; history of, 16–17; youth violence in, 6, 15

entextualization, 53, 70

Evangelical Christianity: concept of sin in, 98, 105, 116; offering sanctuary from violence, 118, 121–125, 128; relationship with gangs, 15, 22, 110–114, 117–118, 121; salvation in, 105–107, 114, 135; youth participation in, 7, 9, 134–135. *See also* conversion; Pentecostal; salvation

evangelizing campaigns, 22, 42–43, 46, 108–109, 118

faith: in base ecclesiastical communities, 81–83; and Catholic youth group, 25, 75; and community, 25, 75, 87–89, 94–95, 99, 105; and evangelizing, 95; and friendship, 83–85; and love, 85–87, 94, 114; Pentecostal concept of, 104, 135; and works, 25, 73, 81, 87–89, 99, 105. *See also* Catholic; conversion; Evangelical Christianity; Pentecostal; salvation

fictive kinship, 53, 56–57, 59. *See also* blood brother; *carnal*

gang members: as perpetrators of crime, 13, 22, 39, 58, 95–96, 118, 135;

rehabilitation of, 91, 95–96, 100; relationship to *cristianos*, 4, 110–113, 121–124, 126; relationship to Evangelical Christianity, 15, 22, 110–114, 117–118, 121; relationship to neighborhood space, 33–36, 39, 41 (*see also* graffiti); relationship with Pentecostals, 22–23, 54, 71, 113, 118, 122–126; social identity as, 5, 8, 53, 59, 65, 120, 124. *See also* blood brother; *carnal*; 18th Street Gang; fictive kinship; graffiti; *mara*; *marero*; *pandilla*; tattoos

Gell, Alfred, 63–65, 144n2

Good Friday services, 43–46

graffiti: in 18th Street Gang, 8, 25, 30, 39–41, 65–66, 68; and memory, 66–67; roll-call, 66–67, 144n5; tags, 8, 25, 27, 30, 38–41, 65; and tattoos, 8, 25, 54, 65, 134; tombstone, 25, 62, 67, 69

Honduras: citizen insecurity in, 19, 24, 48–49, 54, 90–92; foreign debt, 10–11, 16, 89; military, 11–13, 16, 107, 136; religion in, 105, 107, 116–118, 126; and youth policies, 7, 14, 76, 134; zero tolerance laws, 13–14

Hurricane Mitch, 16–17

incarnation, 53, 70

juvenile delinquency, 9–10, 36, 92

Latin American Bishops' Conference (CELAM), 80

Lefebvre, Henri, 8–9, 39

Maduro, Ricardo, 10, 13

making do, 132–135

maquilas, 16, 52, 91–92

mara, 22, 40, 144. *See also* 18th Street
   Gang; gang members; *marero*
marero, 13, 22–23, 91. *See also* 18th
   Street Gang; gang members;
   mara
marijuana, 33, 50, 65, 73, 112
memorialization, 7–8, 45–47, 62–63,
   66–67
military: involvement in politics,
   10–14, 90, 136; patrols, 5, 64, 107
moral community, 9, 25, 78–79,
   93–94, 101
moral panic, 10, 64

neoliberalism: and base ecclesiastical
   communities, 89–92, 100–101; and
   diminished opportunities, 14, 92,
   133–136; and suffering, 11, 106; and
   violence, 89–90, 92, 101, 106, 133;
   and youth, 89–92

pandilla, 40, 144n4
pastoral de acompañamiento, 81–82
path of God, 111, 114–115, 121–122,
   127–128
Pentecostal: concept of salvation,
   23, 46, 107, 120, 135; evangelizing,
   42, 104, 118–119; relationship with
   gangs, 22–23, 54, 71, 113, 118, 122–
   126; separation from society, 19, 26,
   52, 71, 101, 135. *See also* conversion;
   Evangelical Christianity
police: corruption, 12–14; harassment,
   3, 34, 64, 117, 136; patrols, 3, 5, 11,
   24, 64
preferential option for the poor,
   80–81

reputation: of churches, 116, 118; of
   people, 23, 34, 36, 47, 111, 131; of
   places, 18, 27, 30, 33, 36, 47
resilience, 8, 26, 133–135, 138

salvation: in Evangelical Christianity,
   105–107, 114, 135; in Pentecostalism,
   23, 46, 107, 120, 135; relationship to
   violence, 115–116, 125
sanctuary: in Evangelical Christianity,
   118, 121–127; in Pentecostalism,
   26, 101, 121–127; and political refugees, 120, 127; from violence, 9, 26,
   107, 117, 128, 135
San Pedro Sula, 16–19, 38, 90
Second Vatican Council, 80–81
sense of place, 8, 38
sin: social definition of, 81–82, 98, 101
social space, 8, 33, 37, 48, 105, 126–128
solidarity: base ecclesiastical communities and, 81, 89, 100; Catholic
   youth concept of, 75, 88–89, 92,
   94–96, 100; among gang members,
   57; in theology of accompaniment,
   87, 98
space: and graffiti, 41; control over
   public: 8, 36–39, 42, 47–49, 136,
   143n1, 143n2; memorialization of,
   46–47; neighborhood, 18, 29–31, 66,
   136; redefinition of, 30, 37. *See also*
   social space
street socialization, 8, 25, 53–55, 68, 70
structural adjustment policies, 10–11

tattoos: in 18th Street Gang, 2, 8, 25,
   64–65, 134; and graffiti, 8, 25, 54–55,
   65, 134; removal of, 25, 60, 61–63,
   65, 71; and social skin, 62–64, 70; as
   writing practice, 59, 63, 65, 68. *See
   also* Gell, Alfred
theology of accompaniment, 9, 75,
   80–81, 92–96, 100–101; and solidarity, 87–89, 98

Vatican II. *See* Second Vatican
   Council
Vigil, Diego, 8, 25, 53–54

vigilante justice, 13–14, 24

violence: and churches, 42–47, 75, 89, 98, 104–107, 113–114, 121–128, 135; coping with, 6–9, 15, 21, 24–26, 47, 105–107, 132–138; cultural politics of, 9–15; cyclical nature of, 130, 135–136; impact on community, 8, 29–30, 47, 73–76, 94, 98, 100, 118; impact on individual, 5, 11, 43, 71, 105, 130; impact on nation-state, 7, 10, 45, 90, 92, 118; impact on public space, 48–49, 98; impact on youth, 5–7, 15, 29, 134; and neighborhood places, 31–37, 45–47; and neoliberalism, 89–90, 92, 101, 106, 133; as product of social relationships, 30–31, 34–35; and salvation, 115–116, 125; sanctuary from, 9, 25–26, 98, 107, 117, 128, 135; and solidarity, 94; spectatorship of, 2; state level, 81, 107, 128, 136; stories about, 29–31, 36, 46–47; in street peer groups, 56–59; structural conditions of, 26, 90, 92, 133, 135–136

Weber, Max, 125

youth: crime, 3, 7, 9, 22, 30, 91–93; cultural politics of, 9–11, 14, 136; and cultural practice, 12, 15; groups, 9, 21–22, 25, 72–80, 83–90, 93–101, 105; and religious conversion, 21, 23, 25–26, 114, 134, 135; as social actors, 23, 133–135; and violent death, 11, 12, 43, 45, 49–50. *See also* 18th Street Gang; *mara*; *marero*; violence

Zelaya, Manuel, 38

About the Author

Jon Wolseth's primary research interest is in the experience of child-hood and youth at the margins of social life in urban Latin America. His articles have appeared in the *Journal of Latin American and Caribbean Anthropology*, in *Latin American Perspectives*, and as chapters in recent edited volumes on youth violence in Latin America and child learning. After graduating with his PhD from the University of Iowa, he became a Peace Corps volunteer in the Dominican Republic. He spent nearly three years in Santo Domingo as a homeless-youth outreach specialist. This experience forms the basis of his next research project, a narrative ethnography of street kids in Santo Domingo. He teaches anthropology at Luther College.

LaVergne, TN USA
12 January 2011
212193LV00003B/2/P